IMMORTALS OF SCIENCE

ROBERT BOYLE

Founder of Modern Chemistry

by Harry Sootin

Pictures by Gustav Schrotter

Purple House Press
Kentucky

Published by
Purple House Press
PO Box 787
Cynthiana, Kentucky 41031

Classic Books for Kids and Young Adults
purplehousepress.com

Copyright © 2025 by Purple House Press
Written by Harry Sootin in 1962
Cover: *The Hon. Robert Boyle, experimental philosopher.* Oil painting.
Wellcome Collection.

Unabridged
All rights reserved

ISBN 9798888181980 paperback
9798888181997 hardcover

Contents

1. The New Science — 1
2. The Seventh Son — 3
3. Young Lords at Eton — 12
4. Five Years on the Continent — 20
5. The "Invisible College" — 28
6. Laboratory on the High Street — 37
7. *The Spring of the Air* — 54
8. Boyle's Law — 62
9. *The Sceptical Chymist* — 69
10. Flame and Air — 81
11. "The Christian Gentleman" — 93
12. Boyle Returns to London — 105
13. Courageous Invalid — 115

ONE

The New Science

THE SEVENTEENTH CENTURY was a time of turmoil in Europe. Politicians schemed, armies fought, and religious groups clashed. In England, the Puritan Revolution led to the beheading of a king. Many Englishmen emigrated to the New World in the hope of finding peace and freedom.

More important than the struggle for power and land, however, was the revolution in men's thinking that took place during the 1600's. Galileo, the great Italian astronomer and physicist, had shown that knowledge could be acquired by experiment, thus ushering in the scientific era. Soon the experimental method attracted other bold, creative minds. Men began to investigate nature with free, unrestrained curiosity. Other famous scientists of Galileo's time—Johannes Kepler, William Gilbert, and René Descartes—also helped to lay the foundations of modern science.

The Western world was inspired by this "New Science" which offered a fresh way of looking at and thinking about nature. Men lost their reverence for the scientific ideas of the Greeks. They turned away from the methods of the medieval scholars, which was to arrive at "facts" by discussion and logic. Scientists learned to measure, to weigh, to use mathematics—and to ask questions. Facts came first. According to the New Science, nature would provide answers to all questions—if the experimental approach was used.

Furthermore, the new scientific method permitted every man to question the conclusions of other scientists, since all he had to do was to repeat their experiments himself. There was no room for secrecy or mystery in the New Science. Each investigator had the right to make use of the discoveries of other scientists, for all scientific knowledge was now regarded as a common treasure of mankind.

The New Science provided an outlet for the intellectual energy of numerous individuals in Europe and America. Men were inspired by the vision of the new and better world that science would some day create.

Among the great men who worked hard to bring about this revolution in men's thinking during the seventeenth century was Robert Boyle. This outstanding English scientist was the most effective teacher of the experimental method and the founder of modern chemistry.

TWO

The Seventh Son

THERE WAS much excitement one winter afternoon in Lismore Castle, which was only a few miles from the ancient city of Cork, Ireland. Lady Cork had just given birth to her fourteenth child—a boy. Now her husband, Richard Boyle, first Earl of Cork, was the father not of six but of seven sons. The new child, born on January 25, 1627, was christened Robert Boyle in the private chapel of the castle.

Lord Cork regarded himself as a lucky man. He praised God for his good fortune because the boy was healthy and his wife seemed to be doing well. The Earl of Cork was a successful man in every way. He owned huge estates in the province of Munster, which is in southwest Ireland. In the entire country there was no more influential man than Lord Cork. He had first come to Ireland from England to seek his fortune at the age of twenty-two. Now, almost forty years later, he was generally regarded as not only the most important man in Ireland, but also one of the wealthiest persons in the British Isles.

Lord Cork was highly ambitious. To him it was a matter of prime importance that the Boyle name, wealth, and social position should last for a long time—if possible, forever. Cork was convinced of the many advantages of a large family; as a shrewd father he would arrange for his daughters to marry wealthy and important men, and for his sons to marry women of wealthy and prominent families. In this way the Boyle line would grow more and more powerful as time went on.

However, Richard Boyle, the Earl of Cork, was no hero to the Irish. Like many other young Englishmen of that time, he had gone to Ireland to make his fortune in whatever way he could. In an incredibly short time young Boyle became the owner of tens of thousands of acres of the best land in Munster. Energetic and enterprising, he succeeded in building towns, establishing factories, constructing castles, and even organizing a private army. But to the original Irish landowners, Lord Cork was nothing more than a foreign adventurer who had managed to buy up large tracts of land cheaply from the hard-pressed Irish.

Robert, Cork's seventh son, was left under his mother's care for only a few years. Then he was sent to the home of a nearby farmer to be cared for and reared. It was a custom among well-to-do families in that part of the country to send children away from home at an early age for what was called "toughening." Simple food, fresh air, and small inconveniences were supposed to improve the health of a child as well as develop a sturdy character. In addition, the lack of comforts and luxuries during the early years would, it was hoped, make the better things of life more appreciated later.

Lismore Castle

Unfortunately, Robert never really got to know his mother, for she died in Dublin in 1630, about a year after the birth of her fifteenth child. Lady Boyle was only forty-four years of age at her death. Naturally, it was a shock for four-year-old Robert to lose his mother. Indeed, for the rest of his life Robert Boyle regarded her early death as the "chief misfortune of his life."

During his early years at the farmhouse, a coach would be sent on certain days from Lismore Castle to bring little Robert back for a brief visit. On one such occasion the coach carrying Robert and a servant overturned while crossing a swollen stream. Only the prompt action of a passing gentleman in snatching the boy from the swaying coach saved him from drowning.

Robert, who was an unusually serious youngster, took this experience to heart and managed to extract from it an important personal message. It seemed plain to the boy that his miraculous escape from death was nothing less than a warning from Providence about his future conduct. From now on it would be up to him, Robert, to lead a good and worthy life. Had not the coach overturned and been swept downstream as soon as he had been removed from it? Robert was certain that Providence, his own past behavior, and his future conduct were somehow tied together in this rescue.

At the time, no one would have guessed that a member of the Earl of Cork's family would emerge as one of the greatest scientists of the century. The Earl himself had no interest in books—that is, except for the one in which he kept a daily record of his financial transactions. Likewise, Lady Cork, a gentle and beautiful woman, had never pretended to be a person of education; she had mastered reading and writing, but not much more.

Robert Boyle did have one great advantage: his father, who was a man of the world, knew well the value of a good education. At the same time, however, Lord Cork must have been somewhat baffled by Robert because the boy was apparently different from his brothers, who were overfond of horses, money, and society. Yet, for some reason the shrewd, practical, worldly father found himself drawn to the gentle, thoughtful Robert.

How different the boy was from the rest of his family is revealed by an incident that Robert Boyle himself described later in life. Little Robert was once warned by his sister not to eat the plums of one of the trees in the Lismore orchard. The fruit of this particular tree had been promised to someone else in the family. The inevitable happened, however, and Robert's sister discovered her younger brother in the act.

"Didn't I warn you not to go near that tree, Robert?" scolded his sister. "I explained to you that its plums had been promised to our sister-in-law."

"You did warn me," admitted Robert.

"But I saw you eating the plums. You must have eaten six of them."

"I didn't eat six plums," insisted the boy.

"You mean to stand there and deny eating those plums?"

"I don't deny eating the plums. But I deny eating six. I remember eating twenty!"

Lord Cork must have chuckled over the incident. How extraordinary to have a son who not only disliked lying but even regarded it as evil, sinful! Cork loved Robert deeply because the boy was so innocent, so direct, so honest.

As time went on, Lord Cork became more and more convinced that he had a most remarkable youngest son. He decided to treat Robert with great care because his nature and interests were so different and appealing. No expense must be spared in helping the boy develop into an unusual man, a great man. There were, thought Cork, plenty of politicians and businessmen in the world; his son need not become one of them. Robert had something infinitely rarer and more attractive—an unselfish nature, a natural thoughtfulness, a love of learning.

Lord Cork, therefore, hired the most capable of tutors to instruct Robert at home. French was regarded as the language of polite society at this time, and so a Frenchman was given the job of teaching Robert to speak the language fluently. Latin was the universal language of scholars; the chaplain of Lismore Castle undertook to teach the boy Latin.

Robert's father felt a great deal of satisfaction as he watched his son's progress. Unfortunately, Lord Cork never realized that his son at this time was instructing himself in the art of stammering! It seems that Robert, deprived of the care of a watchful mother, found considerable amusement in imitating the halting speech of some of his little friends. As one might have guessed, what began as a bit of fun ended disastrously: Robert played the part of a stammerer so well that he became a stammerer himself. Indeed, this serious speech defect was to handicap him for the rest of his life.

Thus, as Boyle grew older, the embarrassment of speaking with strangers caused him to avoid people as much as possible. And his childhood, spent among uneducated people who did not hesitate to poke fun at a stammerer, was largely an unhappy one. The boy withdrew into himself as the years passed. Very likely this affliction was to a large extent responsible for Robert Boyle's intellectual development. Because he felt uncomfortable with strangers, the fields of work open to him were necessarily limited. Before long it appeared that study, thinking, writing and experimenting were the things that suited him best. Who knows but that Robert Boyle might have been a far different and less creative person if he had not made himself into a stammerer?

When Robert reached eight years of age, Lord Cork decided that the time had come to send his beloved son away once again. The boy's father had definite ideas on how the son of a prominent person should be educated. Ireland, Cork felt, lacked the right intellectual climate: there was too much preoccupation with material things. Also, the English colonizers of Ireland often felt they were sitting on a powder keg—and they were, for hatred, unrest and rebelliousness were everywhere.

Eton College in England, thought Cork, was the place for Robert; the boy needed the discipline of a good school. Francis Boyle, four years older than his brother Robert, could also profit from a few years at Eton. Sending these two to a good school seemed a sensible step to Lord Cork, for of his seven sons only Francis and Robert showed any interest in scholarship. In addition, the Earl also believed that the boys might become lazy, luxury-loving and overproud if they remained in the wealthy atmosphere they were so accustomed to. Off to England they must go.

Lord Cork's ideas about extravagance, however, did not prevent him from buying an estate in England where Robert might some day live and devote himself to his studies. There was nothing like looking ahead, thought the practical-minded nobleman. Doubtless he felt that the gentle, lovable Robert had to be protected from the world, for he realized that this particular son would never become a collector of wealth or of titles. In his simple way, Lord Cork, man of the world and father of a most unworldly son, wanted more than anything else to bring the unusual mind of Robert into bloom.

Soon everything was arranged. The two boys, accompanied by Lord Cork's business agent, their tutor, and their personal valet, Cary, were to board a ship at Youghal, the seaport nearest Lismore. Crossing the Irish Channel to Bristol, England, was no simple matter in those days. The wind had to be just right; and there was the ever-present danger of being intercepted by Turkish pirates, who at that time frequently raided Channel ships.

After a few delays, Robert and Francis made the crossing safely. From Bristol they traveled to Eton by coach, arriving at the famous college on October 2, 1635.

THREE

Young Lords at Eton

THE YOUNG MEN from Ireland soon discovered that life at Eton was quite different from that at home. At Lismore they had enjoyed long pleasant hours between sessions with tutors; here at Eton, however, everything was organized and supervised under the capable administration of Sir Henry Wotton, the Provost, or Superintendent, of the College. Aside from sleeping and dining, students were expected to use almost every precious hour for the improvement of their minds.

They were required to get up before dawn to attend prayer reading, after which came breakfast and two hours of instruction. Next came an hour's recess, which was followed by chapel and then dinner at eleven. From noon to three o'clock, the students applied themselves to their studies. When this was over, the tired scholars were eager for an hour on the playing fields and this was exactly what they got.

But the day was still young. The exercise hour was followed by another hour of instruction and then supper, which was served at five o'clock in the afternoon. Afterward came two hours of preparation for the next day's schoolwork. At seven o'clock, each student was allowed a traditional late snack consisting of bread and beer. By eight in the evening everything was quiet, for the weary Etonians were all in bed.

The two boys from Lismore adjusted to this strict discipline with little difficulty. They liked and respected Sir Henry Wotton. Sir Henry, a cousin of the philosopher Francis Bacon, was no ordinary schoolmaster. He was an excellent scholar, a lover of Italian culture, and an ex-ambassador to Venice.

As sons of nobility, Francis and Robert Boyle were permitted to have a servant of their own—the same Cary who had escorted them from Ireland to Eton. They dined at a table which was honored by the presence of the chaplain and older clerks, all of whom were waited on by some of the poorer students, as was the custom at that time.

This treatment as members of the upper class did not spoil the boys, because it was exactly what they had been used to at home. As the sons of the powerful Earl of Cork, the wealthiest man in England, they were bound to be treated differently from most other students.

The education they received was the best that tradition, care, and money could provide. The Boyles' headmaster, John Harrison, understood the boys and was extremely skillful at arousing the interests of his students in books and ideas. The tutors who did the day-to-day work of teaching were equally capable and just as interested in their charges.

As might have been expected, Robert Boyle took to books like a born scholar. His intense desire to learn plus an unusually retentive memory helped to make him an outstanding student almost at once; soon, Mr. Harrison began to wonder if he had gotten Robert *too* interested in books. The headmaster tried hard to slow his favorite pupil down by insisting that the latter spend more time on the playing fields with other boys. But it was a hopeless effort. Robert had learned to love books and there was little anyone could do about it. The boy was thrilled by all kinds of reading—the classics, poetry, history, and romantic stories.

For the Boyles, the three years at Eton turned out to be pleasant and instructive. Each boy got something out of the experience: Robert—a love for books and learning; Francis—much fun and a taste of knowledge. From all accounts the bookish, serious Robert was well liked by his fellows, despite his superiority as a student. He was kind, gentle, and considerate—traits which must have made him popular with everyone.

As was his growing habit, Robert read a great deal of meaning into the accidents which happened to him. On one occasion, the wall of the room which the two boys occupied fell in while Robert was lying on his bed. Francis was standing nearby talking to a friend when this collapse occurred. Prompt action by the friend in pulling Robert out of the way saved the latter from almost certain death.

On another occasion, Robert was given the wrong medicine by a physician. Fortunately the medicine refused to stay down long enough to do much damage. From then on Robert decided not to depend on careless doctors, but to prescribe his own medicines! Finally, there were two accidents having to do with horses; in each, Robert had a narrow escape from serious injury.

A religious mind like Robert Boyles' could not regard such accidents as merely common occurrences. His escape each time could not be put down to chance or good fortune. Providence was taking care of him, Robert Boyle, because he was leading a good, honest, moral life.

While his two sons were maturing at Eton, Lord Cork, now almost seventy-two years of age, was having his troubles. Like many wealthy and powerful men, he had managed to acquire a number of enemies during his long life. This time his wealth was the main reason for the attack on him by important state and church leaders. The King, Charles I, was in conflict with the English Parliament at this time and needed money in order to strengthen his position. Actually there was nothing personal about the attack launched against Lord Cork: it was simply that he happened to be the man from whom the most money could be extracted.

The enemies of Lord Cork proceeded to levy a huge tax on his properties. Along with this they accused him of appropriating church incomes in Munster. Finally, they claimed that Cork had acquired large areas of land illegally. Soon, the old Earl found it necessary to hurry to England to defend himself against what he regarded as vicious, unfounded charges.

By this time Cork had purchased an estate in Stalbridge, in Dorsetshire, about sixty miles from the port of Bristol, England. Francis and Robert were waiting to greet their father when he arrived there. The troubled Earl found pleasure and comfort in the reunion with his sons, particularly Robert. During the time they had been away from home, the father had received many glowing letters from Cary, the valet, telling about the rapid progress being made by the boys.

The boys were permitted to remain at Eton for a few months longer, and then Lord Cork decided to withdraw them for good in November of 1638. The Earl had a number of reasons for this drastic step. The well-liked Harrison was no longer at the school; Robert had suddenly lost interest in his studies. There was also the danger, according to the Earl's way of thinking, that the boys might learn bad habits and become reckless spenders like their brothers. Lord Cork saw trouble ahead and acted promptly; the boys must be educated at Stalbridge by tutors carefully chosen on the basis of character and learning.

The Earl was a good judge of men as well as an excellent planner. He could see that Francis, at fifteen years of age, was more or less through with schooling. Marriage was what mattered now for the young man. He, Lord Cork, would see to it that the boy found the "right" wife. What the father had in mind, of course, was a marriage contract with a prominent, well-to-do father of an attractive daughter. Lord Cork was an old hand at this type of arranging; he was certain that somewhere he would find a father and daughter who met all the qualifications.

What to do with Robert, the gentle, withdrawn, bookish youth, presented a different kind of problem. There was, however, a parson of excellent education in the nearby village. Why not have Robert board with the parson, who would tutor the boy and supervise his activities? For the Earl it seemed an attractive solution because he would have Robert close to home and be able to see him often. Actually, the aging Lord Cork enjoyed his youngest son so much that he could not bear the thought of sending him off again to a distant school

And so the parson, Mr. W. Douch, proceeded to tutor Robert Boyle for nearly a year. The boy liked his new freedom and really applied himself to his Latin. He had plenty of leisure in which to read and write and dream. In addition, there were frequent trips to Stalbridge manor where he could enjoy the company of his father. Time passed quietly with Robert absorbed in writing verses or trying to untangle ideas during long walks through the countryside.

Then all at once, exciting things began to happen at Stalbridge. King Charles I, who was in the midst of his difficulties with Parliament, found himself confronted by a rebellious Scotland. The First Bishop's War had broken out as a result of the King's insistence that the Scots recognize the authority of certain bishops he had chosen for them. The Scots did not want the King's bishops. To them it was all a plot to undermine the Presbyterian Church of Scotland, and this they determined to resist vigorously—with arms.

The King needed troops desperately. Lord Dungarvan, the Earl of Cork's oldest son, offered to raise a hundred men and lead them into battle against the Scots. Lord Cork, after he had gotten over his anger at not having been consulted, opened his purse strings and furnished the money for equipping the horsemen. In fact, so loyal was the Earl of Cork that he offered five of his sons to the service of his King.

By this time Cork had managed to clear himself of the many charges against him by agreeing to pay 15,000 pounds in three installments to the King's treasury. The Earl thus bought his way back into the good graces of Charles I and was once again regarded as an honest, reliable subject.

At any rate, a few months later peace was restored and Stalbridge began to hum with family activities once more. Before long the Earl started on a project close to his heart—a marriage arrangement for Francis. The lad was almost sixteen and, according to Lord Cork, it was never too early to think about a good match. The father kept looking and soon found what he was looking for: a young girl about fourteen years old, who was well-connected, a maid-of-honor at court, and the daughter of wealthy parents. Her name was Elizabeth Killigrew. There were long negotiations, but this was the sort of thing the Earl was good at. Besides, he had considerable experience making similar arrangements for other sons and daughters.

Since Francis was only sixteen, his father thought it best for the actual marriage to take place two or three years later. His plan now was to send Francis and Robert to the Continent of Europe for the *tour* that every well-to-do Englishman regarded as absolutely essential for a complete education. The King, however, insisted that the marriage take place first.

The King had his way, and on October 24, 1639, Francis and Elizabeth were married with great ceremony. The King and Queen were present and no expense was spared. Four days later Francis, sixteen years old and now a married man, was separated from his bride. He would see her again in a few years, he was told. The important thing now was to hurry and get ready for an educational tour of the Continent. It would not be a lonely trip, for his younger brother Robert would be with him. Together, the two young men would learn about the world beyond England and Ireland.

FOUR

Five Years on the Continent

MONSIEUR MARCOMBES was the name of the Frenchman in whose care Lord Cork decided to place his two sons while they were abroad. The father had complete confidence in this gentleman—and rightly so. An ex-soldier, scholar, and world traveler, Marcombes had recently fulfilled a similar mission for Robert's two older brothers, and all had turned out well. His charges had returned home healthy, mature, and—of extreme importance to the Earl—with their Protestant faith still strong. The present plan was for Francis and Robert to live with the Marcombes at Geneva, Switzerland, for most of the period abroad. The cultured Frenchman was to serve as guardian, advisor, tutor, and interpreter of foreign customs.

There were five persons in the party which crossed the Channel to Dieppe: the two boys, Marcombes, and two servants Lord Cork had sent along to look after the physical comforts of his sons. After a few days in Paris they joined a group of twenty horsemen bound for Lyons. Each traveler was armed with sword and pistol, fully prepared to defend himself against highwaymen. From Lyons they made their way across the mountains of Savoy to Geneva; here the tired youths settled down as boarders of the Marcombes family.

Their tutor took his job seriously and the boys were instructed in Latin, French, fencing, dancing, and fortification. This last subject was considered one that every young English nobleman should learn, particularly if he expected to inherit extensive estates in Ireland. Soon Robert began studying mathematics. He found that he liked arithmetic and geometry, which was somewhat surprising in a dreamy boy so fond of reading French romances.

Lord Cork never really appreciated the extraordinary qualities of the Marcombes. The tutor was blessed with the finest type of French mind; he was logical, keen, and critical. In addition, the Frenchman believed in thrift, had a sharp sense of humor, and detested deception and showiness. The innocent, dreamy Robert learned a great deal from Marcombes and was forever grateful to the intelligent, honest tutor. As for Francis, Marcombes' influence must have been less important, for the youth's thoughts were naturally concerned with the young wife waiting for him in England.

At that time there was an unusually tolerant religious atmosphere in Geneva, the center of Presbyterianism. The many prominent Catholics who resided there felt free to argue and discuss matters with their Calvinist neighbors. Robert, who was naturally religious, found the debates exciting. He plunged into a study of the Bible and began to teach himself Hebrew,

Aramaic, and Syriac, which together with Latin and Greek enabled him to read the ancient texts.

While at Geneva, Robert had a religious experience which, he said later, was the "considerablest of his whole life." It happened during a violent summer thunderstorm when the frightened boy awakened to peals of thunder, dazzling bolts of lightning, howling winds, and a tremendous downpour. Robert, convinced "of the day of judgment's being at hand," trembled at the thought that perhaps he was not yet prepared to meet it. The next day, bright and clear, found the boy more determined than ever to live a blameless, religious life.

After living in Geneva for about two years, the Boyle brother became restless. There were so many more interesting places in Europe they longed to visit—if only Lord Cork would give his permission. They kept writing home asking to be allowed to go to Italy. Their father was reluctant...Englishmen were not safe in Italy...the boys might be influenced by the Catholicism of Rome. Finally the Earl yielded and brought great joy to his sons in Geneva; preparations immediately began for the Italian journey.

In September of 1641, accompanied by Marcombes, they crossed the Alps on horseback, paused at Venice, made their way across the plains of Lombardy, and eventually reached the beautiful city of Florence. As it happened, the Boyles were in Florence when Galileo died in nearby Arcetri on January 8, 1642.

During the winter they remained in Florence, where Robert studied the works of Galileo. He quickly became an ardent admirer of the famous Italian scientist. The Copernican system, revealing experiments, new mechanics, a fresh approach to nature—all these impressed the imaginative Robert Boyle and helped turn his ambitions in a new direction.

Spring came and the visitors decided to move on to Rome, where there were so many ancient monuments to see. By this time Robert had learned to speak French fluently, almost as well as a Frenchman. Since English Protestants were, at that time, not made to feel welcome in Rome, Robert decided to masquerade as a Frenchman. He would then be able to move about freely in Rome without fear of unpleasant incidents. This he managed to carry off successfully.

After an instructive few weeks in Rome, the Boyles returned to Florence and from there journeyed to Livorno, where a sailboat was hired to take them first to Genoa and then along the Riviera to France. In May of 1642, the party reached Marseilles, where they expected to find waiting for them money from home together with permission to return to England.

But in Marseilles they found neither money nor a letter from Lord Cork. What were they to do? For several days they marked time anxiously; the boys soon found themselves depending on Marcombes' limited funds for food and lodging. At last a letter came from Ireland with a depressing account of all the difficulties their father was having in rebellious Munster. As for money, Lord Cork could spare only 250 pounds for his sons; there would be no more for a long time because he needed every pound for the defense of his embattled estates in Ireland.

Most serious of all to the youthful Boyles was the sad fact that even this money never reached them. What were they to do—two young English noblemen stranded in southern France without funds? Lord Cork had suggested that Marcombes help his sons get to a safe Irish port. But with what? They had no money at all, and the cost of getting his charges to Ireland was beyond the tutor's small resources.

However, there was no holding Francis Boyle, who was now nearing nineteen years of age. He simply had to get back to Ireland as quickly as possible. Francis felt that his place was alongside his father and brothers, who were fighting desperately for their lives and properties. With the help of the ever-reliable Marcombes, they got enough money together for Francis' passage, and off to Ireland the older brother sailed.

At this point Robert Boyle, exhausted by the long journey from Italy and worried over his father's troubles, became ill. Marcombes managed to convince young Boyle that a tired, ailing fifteen-year-old boy would be of little help to Lord Cork's army. It soon became clear that the most sensible thing for Marcombes and Robert to do was to return to Geneva at once and wait there for developments in England. Perhaps the situation would soon change for the better. Or, if Robert recovered rapidly he could still join the fighting forces of his father later.

Unfortunately for Lord Cork, things did not improve. The long struggle between Charles I and Parliament had encouraged the Irish to rebel once again. The time seemed right to the Irish leaders, for Charles I was so busy coping with the Great Rebellion at home that he could not spare an army to suppress the rebellion in Ireland.

Thus, in 1641, with arms and funds obtained on the Continent, the furious Irish had launched an assault on the English estates in Ulster. In a short time, they were in control of most of that province. From there, the revolt had spread to other parts of the country and soon reached Munster, where Lord Cork was making a strong stand at Lismore Castle. With his sons at his side and a well-trained private army under his command, Lord Cork managed to drive off the Irish time and time again.

The seventy-six-year-old Earl of Cork was a fighter and refused even to consider surrendering to the rebels. He felt certain that, given enough time, he could drive the Irish army out of Munster. In the meantime, he intended to hold out as well as he could. Unexpectedly, however, matters were taken out of his hands. He received a communication from the King stating that a peace treaty was about to be signed with the Irish. At the same time, the King asked Lord Cork to declare a brief truce in the fighting at Lismore.

It was a bitter experience for the aged Earl, for he realized that the King's negotiations with the Irish rebels meant official recognition of their grievances and the permanent curtailment of his own power in Ireland. Soon after this blow, the Earl of Cork died, a broken and disappointed man.

At Geneva, meanwhile, Robert Boyle was nursed back to health by the faithful Marcombes, who continued to board and teach the young Englishman without payment. Boyle's diary tells little about this second period in Geneva, but apparently he made the best of the situation and devoted himself to his studies. He must have had many anxious days as he tried to read between the lines of the news items that filtered through to Switzerland.

England at this time was engaged in the bloody struggle between the Royalist upper classes, who were nicknamed the "Cavaliers," and the Puritan middle classes, called the "Roundheads." Since the Puritan-dominated "Long Parliament" controlled London, the King found it necessary to move to Oxford. All of Robert's brothers were, of course, on the side of the Royalists and prepared to make every sacrifice for their king.

Poor Robert Boyle did not know what to do, or to whom to turn. How long could he continue to live with Monsieur Marcombes and accept his charity? He was aware by this time that his father had died, broken in spirit and probably ruined financially. Also, it was now two years since Francis had separated from him, and almost five years since both had set out from England.

The young Englishman was determined to get home somehow. With the help of Marcombes and some money obtained by the sale of a "few slight jewels," Robert managed to scrape together the necessary passage money. All preparations having been made, he said good-bye to his generous tutor, promising to repay all that the latter had spent on his support.

The summer of 1644 found Robert Boyle alone and penniless in London. He was seventeen years old and on his own. There was no longer a fond, wealthy father to turn to for help. For, according to all reports, Lord Cork's vast empire in Munster had been completely destroyed.

FIVE

The "Invisible College"

IT IS NOT known how long the lonely Robert Boyle wandered about the streets of London feeling and thinking like a foreigner. His world had been turned upside down while he was away. The city itself seethed with unrest and violence. Cavaliers and Roundheads were hurriedly preparing for the decisive battle at Marston Moor, which was to take place that very year, 1644.

According to Boyle's own account, he met his sister Katherine, Lady Ranelagh, by mere accident in London. As one might expect, he immediately interpreted this stroke of luck as further evidence that Providence was looking out for him. Katherine, though several years older than he, was Boyle's favorite sister. She lived in London, had many intellectual interests, and was the only member of the Boyle family who sympathized with the Puritan cause. More important for Robert, however, was the fact that his sister had become a trusted friend of many of the most prominent scientists and political figures of the time.

As a result of her father's excessive enthusiasm for a financially sound marriage arrangement, she had married at sixteen. But her husband, Arthur Jones, eldest son of Viscount Ranelagh, proved to be a crude, violent-tempered, seldom sober mate. Even Lord Cork must have realized that the marriage was a cruel mistake. The bright sensitive girl suffered silently for many years and finally convinced her troublesome husband that it would be best for her to leave Ireland and live in London—by herself. Not many years later her husband died and Katherine was free at last to live the civilized intellectual life for which she had always yearned.

Katherine was overjoyed at finding her brother safe in London. She insisted that he live in her spacious house in Pall Mall. There she nursed him back to health and helped plan his future. Robert was her favorite brother and there had long been a strong bond between these two most intelligent members of the Boyle family.

From his sister, Robert Boyle learned that the political situation of his family was not as hopeless as he had thought. First, Katherine had many important friends in Parliament, and these could be relied upon to help him, despite the fact that the other Boyles were fighting on the side of the Royalists. Then there was the extraordinary position of their older brother, Lord Broghill, whose continued resistance in Munster against the sweep of the Irish rebels had made him a hero to Cavaliers and Roundheads alike. Apparently the only idea about which both sides in the English Civil War could agree was that Ireland must be held at all costs for the honor and profit of England.

The news about Francis Boyle proved depressing, however. The young man had plunged into the Irish struggle on his return from the Continent two years earlier and was still involved in it. His young wife simply refused to join her husband in Ireland, for she preferred the excitement of the Court and would not leave it despite Francis' pleas.

Katherine felt truly sorry for Francis. She knew, from her own unhappy experience, what his state of mind must be. Indeed, both Katherine and Francis did not have to be convinced that their late father had been skillful in arranging unhappy marriages. Katherine was also aware that even Robert would not have escaped the farseeing plans of Lord Cork, had the Earl lived a few years longer. For, when the boy was only twelve Lord Cork already had picked a "likely" wife for his favorite son—the daughter of a prominent and wealthy nobleman. While Robert Boyle was in Geneva, however, the young lady married someone else and thus the Earl's planning had come to nothing.

Besides, now that Robert Boyle was back in England, he had many matters on his mind—and romance was definitely not one of them. What he wanted more than anything else at this time was to stay out of the civil war, a conflict he regarded as barbaric and senseless. If only he could get back to the beautiful estate in Stalbridge, where he could live a quiet, studious life until peace returned to his country!

Katherine did not think this was as impossible as it sounded. She was certain that her friends could get permission from

Parliament for Robert to travel to the estate in Dorsetshire. Lady Ranelagh, however, cautioned her brother not to expect Stalbridge to be the same lovely place he remembered, for it was quite possible that the manor had been ruined by the warring factions.

During his stay in London with his sister, Robert Boyle became interested in science. Since Lady Ranelagh's social circle included some of the finest scholars in England, Robert naturally came into contact with these outstanding men. Among them were "worthy persons inquisitive into natural philosophy and other parts of human learning." Gradually this group, which included teachers, doctors, astronomers, mathematicians, and interested laymen, began to meet regularly to discuss the New Science.

Still only eighteen years of age in 1645, Boyle would listen wide-eyed to the scientific discussions of his sister's distinguished guests. To him there was something beautiful about the scientific approach to knowledge. Boyle had studied Francis Bacon's works and was aware of the latter's stress on fact, experiment, and observation.

There were other reasons, too, for the favorable impact of the New Science on Boyle—the "goodness" of it, the desire to improve the lot of mankind, the hopefulness of the new knowledge. In short, since humanity was involved, the religious mind of Boyle was strongly attracted by the experimental approach to knowledge.

Before long the young man forgot to be silent and found himself asking questions and even taking part in the learned discussions. The devotees of science must have been impressed by the gentle, charming manners of this serious-minded youth. Soon Boyle's unfortunate stammer was forgotten; only his keenness of mind, enthusiasm, and interest were noticed by the scholarly guests. Later, Boyle was invited to become a member of the group and to attend informal meetings at various places—private homes, Gresham College, and, at times, a well-known tavern.

This was indeed an extraordinary opportunity for Robert Boyle. He resolved to learn all he could about mathematics, mechanics, and chemistry in order to keep up with the group—which he liked to call the "invisible college."

It must be remembered that Boyle never attended a university and that what he had learned about "natural philosophy"—the general term for the sciences—had come chiefly from books. For the young man to be accepted as an equal by the most learned scholars of the period speaks well indeed for his intellect. How much of his mature, keen grasp of the world he owed to Marcombes' influence is difficult to estimate. There is little doubt, however, that association with his French tutor had benefited the dreamy, bookish Robert Boyle.

After he had remained in London for a year, Boyle, with the permission of Parliament, left England again for a brief visit to Geneva. He had not forgotten his debt to Marcombes, with whom he had been corresponding, and the primary purpose of the trip was to repay the money Marcombes had lent him. The tutor, who happened to be in financial difficulties at this time, was touched by Boyle's continued friendship and sense of responsibility.

Before returning home, the young Englishman, now an ardent scientist, purchased a small chemical furnace, which he needed for the experiments he had in mind. Happily, Boyle was now no longer worried about money problems, for Parliament, thanks to his sister's influence, had agreed to allow him to receive the income from the English properties.

Back in London, Boyle was faced with an important question: How long could he afford to live away from Stalbridge, where his large estate was so in need to capable management? In 1646, Boyle made up his mind that property matters could no longer be put aside; he would simply have to settle down at Stalbridge and devote himself to managing the estate his father had left him. Accompanied by his brother, Lord Broghill, for part of the journey, Boyle succeeded in reaching the family manor without being attacked by any of the roving bands of armed men so feared by travelers during the English civil war. Luckily, the safe-conduct pass and messenger provided by the London authorities protected him from being molested by Puritan soldiers.

Boyle was not surprised to find Stalbridge in a state of confusion. Farms and orchards had been completely neglected;

the main house and the tenants' cottages were sadly in need of repair. The young man who had for so long been absorbed in the world of ideas had much to do.

Almost overnight Boyle had to transform himself into an estate manager—a man of business. He found himself confronted by many practical problems: rents, repairs, plowing, planting, and bookkeeping. Although Boyle disliked this type of work, he realized that it had to be done—and done well. It was important that the estate be managed sensibly, profitably. Was it not his duty to improve these properties and make them income-producing? If he, Robert Boyle, should leave no heirs, Francis would inherit Stalbridge. And he was determined to protect the interests of his brother.

The six long years spent at Stalbridge turned out to be quiet and monotonous. Robert Boyle devoted a good deal of his leisure to writing essays on various subjects, among which religion was his favorite. He also studied mathematics and chemistry to prepare himself for a career in experimental science—if he should ever manage to get away from Stalbridge. Actually, Boyle felt restless because of a deep-seated feeling that his life was being wasted on unimportant practical matters when there were so many other things he wanted to do. Every now and then, the bored young man would break away from the unbearable routine and rush off to London to attend the exciting meetings of the "invisible college."

Always he would return refreshed and eager to learn more about the subjects he had heard discussed, or the experiments he had seen performed. Before long, however, boredom would set in again. Perhaps because he had too much time on his hands, Boyle during this period began to be intensely concerned with his health. His ailments were not all imaginary, for at the age of twenty he was already experiencing sharp pains from a stone in the kidney. In addition, his eyesight began to fail and he could not help thinking that he might some day go blind. Boyle even made a study of the effects of drugs on his various diseases—both real and imaginary—and took to trying different "cures" on himself. A few earlier unhappy experiences with doctors had convinced him that nothing he tried could be worse than the crude remedies prescribed by the physicians of his century.

If only the civil war would end and things return to normal! Boyle waited and hoped. During the six dismal years at Stalbridge great changes had come about in England. Charles I had been put to death and a Commonwealth established, with Cromwell as the leading military and political personality. The rebellious Irish had been crushed after a campaign of unsurpassed brutality on the part of Cromwell's army.

Lord Broghill, Robert Boyle's brother, though loyal to the Cavaliers, had been compelled to take part in the Irish expedition because of the brilliant campaign he had conducted against the rebels in Munster. Cromwell had offered Broghill a choice: either join the Commonwealth forces in Ireland, or be executed. Broghill decided that fighting the Irish was preferable to death. He did, however, make it clear that under no circumstances would he participate in the war in England against his Royalist friends. Cromwell agreed to this stipulation.

The eventual defeat of the Irish rebels was followed by the restoration to the original owners—provided they were politically "safe"—of estates seized in the Rebellion of 1642. Thanks to Broghill, the Boyle family recovered its immense properties in Munster. In 1652, Robert Boyle found it necessary to go to Ireland to set his huge estates in order.

Thus, as far as Boyle's scientific studies were concerned, two more precious years were wasted. But Boyle was not unhappy, for he was beginning to see a way out. Once this last batch of business details had been attended to, his income would be large and secure. He would be his own master. Soon he would be in a position to forget about property and management problems. Boyle decided not to return to Stalbridge, where he had wasted so much time. He had other plans—exciting ones.

SIX

Laboratory on the High Street

ON HIS return from Ireland, Robert Boyle began to act like a young man in a hurry. Although he had lost much time, he now had a definite goal in life and an intense desire to begin moving toward it at once. In London he discovered that his beloved "invisible college" had been disbanded because of political conditions. Some members had drifted off to Oxford; others were still living in London; a few had simply lost interest in the weekly meetings.

Boyle discussed the situation with Dr. John Wilkins, who had recently been appointed Warden of Wadham College, Oxford. Wilkins encouraged Boyle to settle in Oxford rather than London, pointing out that several members of the invisible college were already holding meetings in the university town. Boyle considered the matter for a while and finally decided that Oxford would indeed be a suitable place in which to do his work.

There was still much to do, however, before Boyle could free himself of vexing property problems. When all the arrangements had been completed, he found that his estates would yield about 3,000 pounds a year in income—a huge sum in those days. He transferred the ownership of Stalbridge to his brother Francis, in the meantime placing that estate in the hands of a trustworthy agent.

After all the business details had been attended to, Boyle rented a suite of rooms in Oxford from a Mr. Crosse, an apothecary whose house on the High Street adjoined University College. Boyle's sister Katherine came up from London to inspect the lodgings and took pains to advise her brother on such matters as which room was likely to be most comfortable and "not have the inconvenience of wind." Boyle set up a complete, no-expense-spared laboratory in his suite, installing apparatus from Stalbridge as well as new equipment purchased in London.

In the year 1654, Robert Boyle, at the age of twenty-seven, was at last ready to embark on the career he had long dreamed of—that of an experimental scientist. Here at Oxford, where he was destined to spend fourteen happy and productive years, Boyle had everything one could ask for. He was near his many friends—prominent doctors, chemists, astronomers, mathematicians, and religious leaders. He had money enough not only to employ a laboratory staff but also to buy the finest available apparatus for this research.

Up to this time Boyle had merely dabbled in science. Now that the experimental approach to knowledge was at last open to him, he insisted on learning as much as he could about practical chemistry. For this purpose he engaged a well-known chemist, Peter Stahl, originally from the city of Strasbourg, to instruct him and his staff in the art of manipulating apparatus and other techniques of the laboratory. Always eager to acquire knowledge, whether from books or experts, Boyle was never reluctant to admit his own ignorance.

A year after moving to Oxford, Boyle employed a young man named Robert Hooke as laboratory assistant. It proved a most fortunate choice, for the brilliant Hooke, eight years younger than his employer, turned out to be an imaginative experimenter and a most skillful manipulator of apparatus. In addition, Hooke possessed the intellect and resourcefulness which were destined to make him one of the leading scientists of his century.

Boyle did not publish any scientific papers during his first six years at Oxford. In 1660, however, he announced many discoveries to the world all at once. Undoubtedly there must have been considerable trial-and-error work during those first few years. Moreover, with the inquisitive Boyle and the resourceful Hooke working together in a well-equipped laboratory, there must have been very little wasted time.

Soon after setting up his laboratory, Boyle learned of a pump, invented in 1654 by Otto von Guericke, Burgomaster of Magdeburg, Germany, which was used for "emptying glass vessels." Realizing the importance of this unusual device, Boyle suggested to Hooke that it might be a good idea to try to build one like it. Before long, Hooke, working with Boyle, succeeded in making an air pump superior to von Guericke's in that it did not have to be operated under water. Soon after this triumph, Hooke constructed a second pump which proved even more efficient than the first.

Robert Boyle, in his first published work, merely mentions the pump as a preliminary to important experiments. Later, however, the pump received considerable notice and began to be called Boyle's Pump. But in the second edition of his book, Boyle took pains to give credit to Robert Hooke for a leading part in its construction.

Boyle's improved air pump was like a modern bicycle pump, but with the valves reverse; in other words, it drew air out of a chamber instead of compressing or forcing air in. Also, in Boyle's pump, the valves did not open and close automatically; they had to be worked by hand, one being opened and the other closed at the beginning of each stroke.

The accompanying diagram shows the main idea behind Boyle's method of exhausting, or removing, air from a globe, which he called a "receiver." Boyle first set the oiled leather washer of the piston in a position near the top of the pump barrel, as shown. He wanted to remove the first barrelful of air from the large globe. The brass plug was turned until it closed the opening into which it fit snugly. Then the stopcock leading to the globe was turned to an open position. Up to this point the air had not been affected in any way.

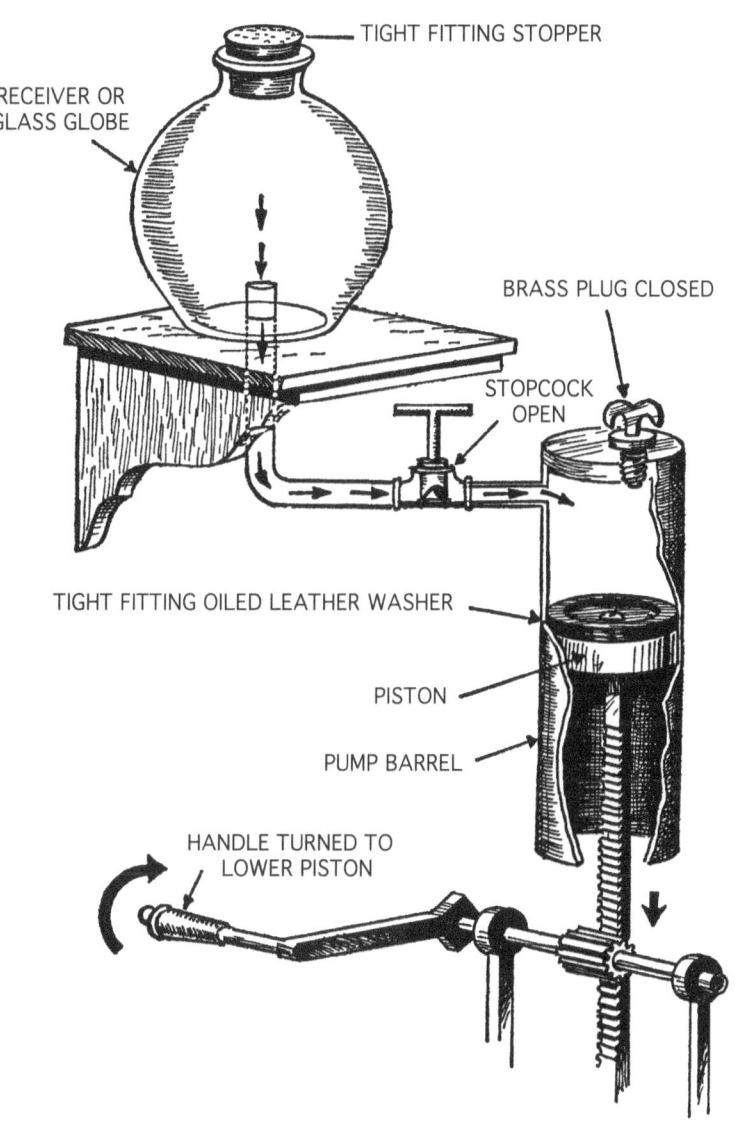

How Boyle's air pump worked. Diagram shows air being drawn out of receiver on downstroke.

Next, Boyle or an assistant pulled the piston down by applying force to the handle. This enlarged the space above the leather washer, causing the air above the washer to thin out and lose pressure. Immediately some of the air from the globe rushed out through the open stopcock into the space above the washer. Why? Because air moved from the higher pressure in the globe to the lower pressure in the pump barrel.

The operator now proceeded to close the stopcock and open the brass plug by turning it. A barrel full of air had been removed from the globe and this air had to be pushed out of the barrel into the air of the room. On the upstroke, the piston rose in the barrel and pushed the air out through the opening at the brass plug.

It took a downstroke and an upstroke to remove one barrelful of air from the globe. Another downstroke and upstroke and a second barrel of air would leave the globe. During each downstroke the stopcock was opened for air to be drawn into the pump barrel; during each upstroke the brass plug was opened to let air out of the pump barrel. The stopcock and brass plug were never opened or closed *at the same time*.

The more strokes, the more air was exhausted or drawn from the globe and therefore the "higher" the resulting vacuum. Today this seems like a crude device to us, but in Boyle's time his pump was regarded as a marvelous invention. The very idea of removing air from a confined space was revolutionary; it raised questions about ideas which had been accepted by philosophers and alchemists for many centuries.

Now that Boyle had a pump capable of exhausting not all, but most, of the air from a receiver, what use could he make of it? Boyle was unusually ingenious and imaginative; he had a boyish desire to try things no one had ever attempted before—at least so far as he knew.

Boyle found plenty of experimental uses for his air pump. For example, he had his glass blowers make a huge receiver, one capable of holding about thirty "wine quarts" and shaped so that the top could be sealed after apparatus had been lowered through it. Boyle was now prepared to carry out some new and interesting experiments.

Why not place a lamb's bladder in the receiver and see what happened when the air in the bladder was exhausted—the receiver, of course, having been sealed. Since it was still many years before rubber balloons were available, animal bladders—soft, elastic, and airtight—were frequently used in experiments. Boyle forced enough air into the bladder to round it out; then he tied its neck securely with thread and suspended the bladder in the receiver.

With every downstroke of the piston, air left the receiver, causing the bladder to swell noticeably. Soon the bladder became so distended that it burst. Boyle was satisfied with the result; namely, that as the air around the bladder became rarefied, or thinned out, the air locked in the bladder began to push outward. In other words, the amount of space occupied by the air inside the bladder depended on the air pressure around it.

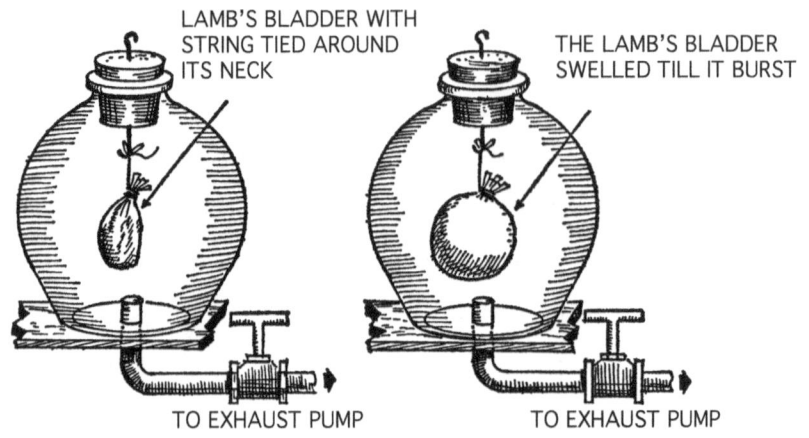

Left: Before exhausting air. Right: While exhausting air.

Boyle next asked himself if substances would burn in a vacuum. This question was soon answered. He passed a wire through the stopper of his receiver. A lighted candle was attached to this wire and then lowered into the globe. The stopper was pushed into place and the candle was allowed to burn until it went out by itself. In this way Boyle learned how long a candle would burn in a closed receiver. The stale air was then blown out of the receiver, fresh air was permitted to flow in, and the candle was relit. This time Boyle immediately began pumping the air out and found that the flame was extinguished much sooner. It was therefore evident that a candle would not burn for as long in a partial vacuum as in air.

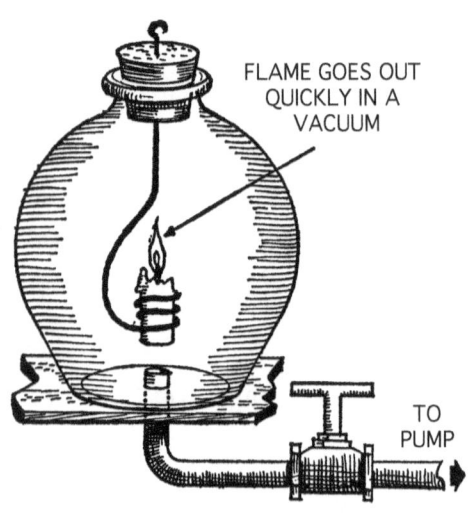

It must be remembered that Boyle's pump could not remove all of the air; enough remained in the receiver to keep the flame burning for about half a minute.

Would a magnet, or lodestone, act through a vacuum? Boyle proceeded to find out. He set a compass needle on a block of wood in his receiver. Before pumping any air out he observed that a magnet brought close to the wall of the receiver attracted or repelled the compass needle inside. Next Boyle pumped as much air as he could out of the receiver and tried the outside magnet again. There was no noticeable difference; the lodestone attracted or repelled the ends of the needle as before. It was plain, therefore, that magnetic forces could pass through a vacuum.

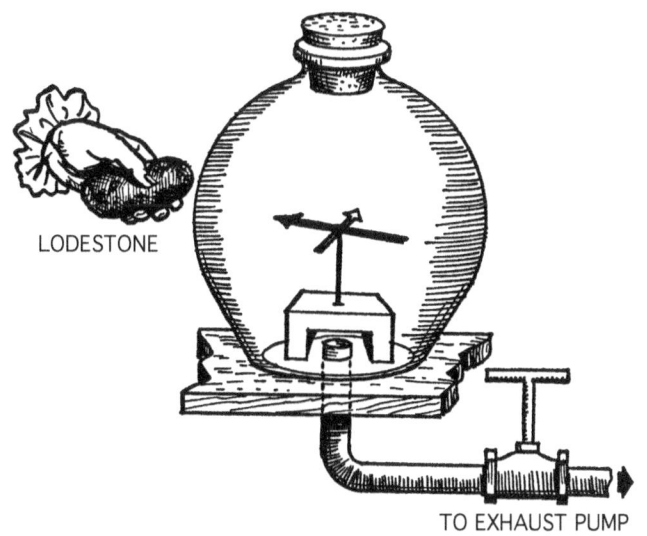

Magnets act through a vacuum.

Boyle made numerous other experiments like these. Some gave interesting, important results. Others didn't prove anything, and some failed entirely. He ran into a few small problems, too. Air, for example, would leak into the pump barrel through the leather washer; the sealing wax around the large stopper at the top of the receiver would crack and allow air to get in. Compared with later vacuum pumps his machine was extremely inefficient. Still, he worked with what he had and made the best of it.

About this time, Boyle's thoughts turned to Torricelli's famous experiment "touching a vacuum," which had been performed by the noted Italian scientist about fifteen years earlier, in 1643. Torricelli had taken a three-foot length of glass tubing, closed at one end, and carefully filled it with mercury. He then pressed his thumb against the open end and inverted the tube in a dish of mercury. The mercury in the tube dropped until it was 30 inches above the level of the mercury in the dish. And there, at the 30-inch mark on that particular day, it stayed.

Torricelli had thus made the first mercury barometer, but exactly why the mercury column remained in the tube was a matter that caused endless arguments among scientists. According to Torricelli, the pressure of the ocean of air above the mercury in the dish kept the column of mercury in place. Today we know that the Italian scientist's view was the correct one.

Five years later, in 1648, Blaise Pascal, the great French scientist, had his brother-in-law set up a mercury barometer on the Puy-de-Dôme, a tall mountain in central France. It was then observed that the barometer level was a few inches lower on a mountain than at sea level. Thus Pascal felt he had proved conclusively that the pressure of the atmosphere was responsible for holding up the mercury in a barometer tube.

Boyle, now that he was in possession of an air pump, undertook to use it to destroy, once and for all, the old idea inherited from Aristotle that "nature utterly abhors a vacuum." At the same time he hoped to prove experimentally that the external pressure of the ocean of air is what keeps mercury at a certain level in a barometer tube.

Boyle gave much thought to planning this experiment. A barometer would have to be placed in the receiver. But how? The three-foot glass tube was too long even for his largest receiver.

Before long, however, Boyle and his assistants hit on a way of doing the experiment. Instead of a large bowl of mercury they would use a small cylindrical "box" of mercury just big enough to get through the narrow opening of the receiver. The barometer tube was filled and inverted in the "box" of mercury; this was done, of course, outside the receiver. A slip of paper, with inches ruled on it, was pasted on the outside of the tube. Then the barometer, with tube held flush against the bottom of the box of mercury, was "by strings carefully let down into the receiver." The next job was to plug up the opening where the tube passed through the stopper, so that no air could leak in. This was done with sealing wax.

Now everything was ready. Before pumping air out of the receiver, Boyle read the barometer level. It was 29.5 inches with the lower part of the barometer in the closed receiver. But this was exactly what the barometer level had been before the instrument had been let down into the receiver.

Why should a sealed-in barometer read exactly the same as an exposed barometer? A few scientists had expected this to be so; but many had argued that the mercury level must fall as soon as the dish of mercury was closed off from the atmosphere. Boyle had already found out something of importance: the barometer level was not immediately affected by enclosing the lower part of the instrument.

It had not been difficult to convince most scientists that the atmosphere pressed down on the mercury in the dish and thus supported the column in the barometer tube. That seemed reasonable. But how could the atmosphere bear down on the dish of mercury in an air-tight globe? A few men, like Boyle and Hooke, could understand that the air in a closed container was under the same pressure as the air in an open one. In the former case, the glass walls kept the air within from expanding; in the latter; the weight of the atmosphere kept the air on the surface of the earth from expanding.

The result in each case was the same: in any particular place on the earth, merely covering a bottle of air did not in any way change the air pressure inside the bottle. As Boyle put it, "When the air is shut into the receiver it doth continue there as strongly compressed, as it did whilst all the incumbent cylinder of the atmosphere leaned immediately upon it."

Boyle was now ready to try the all-important third part of the experiment. It was a tense moment in the laboratory of Mr. Crosse's house when all possible leakage points and been inspected and the pumping was about to start. Boyle's assistant pulled the piston down. The first barrelful of air was drawn from the receiver.

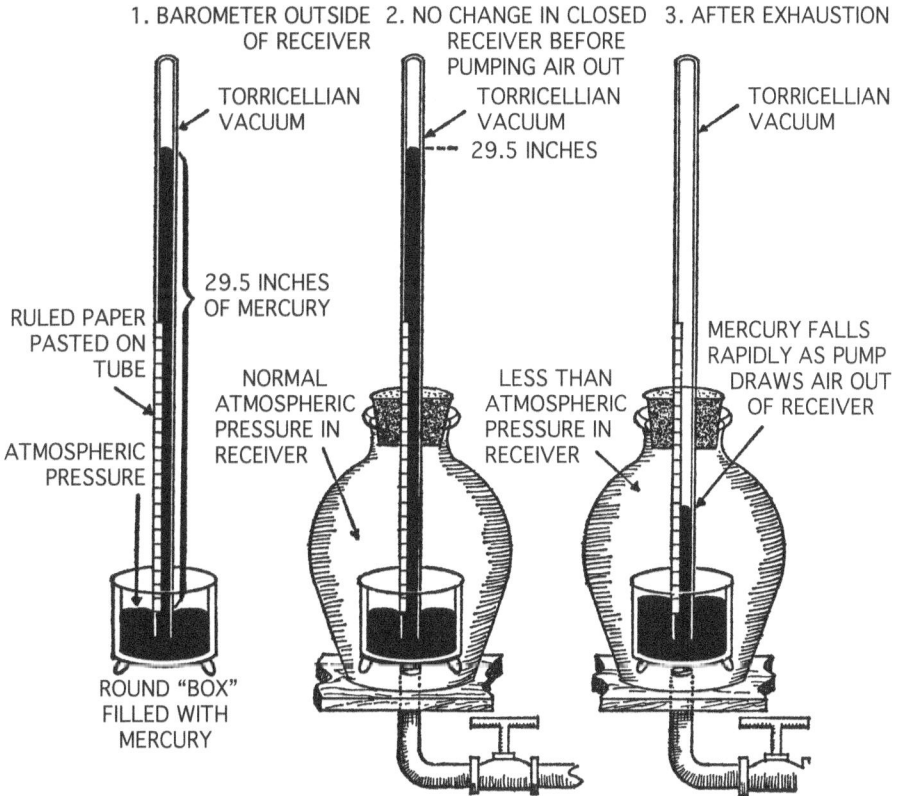

How Boyle showed that the pressure of the atmosphere maintains the mercury in a barometer tube.

Everyone present strained forward to see what happened to the mercury in the long tube. It dropped three-eights of an inch! Another downstroke and the mercury column fell an equal distance.

What better proof that the pressure of air on the surface of the mercury in the "box" supported the mercury column? As the pumping continued, the mercury in the tube "sunk below the top of the receiver, so that we could henceforth mark it in no other way than by the eye." For fifteen minutes Boyle and his assistants continued to pump air out of the receiver, hoping to get every bit of mercury to leave the long tube. But the last half inch or so of mercury proved too much for the pump. To get all of the mercury out would have required a vacuum in the receiver equal to the Torricellian vacuum in the tube. At this point, the outside pressure on the barometer would be zero and therefore the length of the mercury in the tube would also be zero. This his pump simply could not do. Besides, with each stroke the small quantity of air remaining in the receiver seemed to bubble through the last half-inch of mercury to weaken the vacuum within the tube itself.

Robert Boyle, however, was quite happy over his results. He had proved conclusively that in a mercury barometer there existed a balance, or state of equilibrium: the downward pressure of the mercury in the long tube was exactly equal to the opposing pressure of the air on the mercury in the "box." In short, the pressure of the atmosphere and not nature's "dislike or abhorrence" of a vacuum was the true reason why liquids rose in evacuated tubes.

"To satisfy ourselves further" the experimenters proceeded to let the air back into the receiver, a little at a time. The moment the stopcock was opened, air rushed into the receiver and the mercury rose in the tube. When the stopcock was closed to stop the inflow of air, the mercury also stopped rising. In this way they gradually brought the mercury *almost* up to the original level of 29.5 inches. The stopcock was wide open now, but there was no further change in the mercury level. Boyle was able to explain this slight loss in height of the mercury: he remembered that earlier in the experiment some air bubbles had entered the mercury itself and made their way up the tube.

Boyle regarded this experiment as so important that he repeated it before three friends—Christopher Wren, the famous architect, and Dr. John Wallis and Dr. Seth Ward, both distinguished mathematicians. Each of these gentlemen not only "honored it with his presence," but acted as a "judicious witness."

Boyle also performed a noteworthy experiment with the pump itself. He decided to test the power or *efficiency* of the pump. How "high" a vacuum could it produce in comparison with the almost perfect Toricellian vacuum at the top of a barometer tube?

The energetic Boyle "procured several tin pipes about an inch in bore" which he had "soldered together to make one tube about 32 feet long." He then "cemented a strong pipe of glass" about three feet long to the end of the tin pipe. Finally, by means of an "elbow of tin," the long tube was connected to the air pump.

A house of convenient height was selected and a tank of water was placed in the street outside. The pump was on the roof of the house, and the long tube ran from the water tank on the street to the pump on the roof.

Boyle read his mercury barometer. On that particular day it stood $29\frac{1}{4}$ inches high. Since mercury was 14 times heavier than water, the air pressure should raise the water to 14 times the barometer height. Multiplying $29\frac{1}{4}$ inches by 14 gave a figure of close to 34 feet, 2 inches.

How close to this height could Boyle's pump raise water? His assistants pumped and pumped. They got the water up into the glass tube. After twenty "executions" the water rose no higher than 33 feet, 6 inches. This was 8 inches short of the calculated height. Boyle was pleased with the performance of his pump: it had produced a fairly good vacuum. Also, he suspected that mercury was closer to $13\frac{3}{4}$ than to 14 times heavier than water. Boyle's quaint conclusion was that "hence appears the impossibility of making water pass over the highest mountain by help of inflected pipes, and suction."

By this, Boyle probably wanted to make it clear to enthusiasts that his air pump could not be used to transport water from lowlands to hilly areas. The pressure of the atmosphere was capable of raising water 34 feet at most—and no higher.

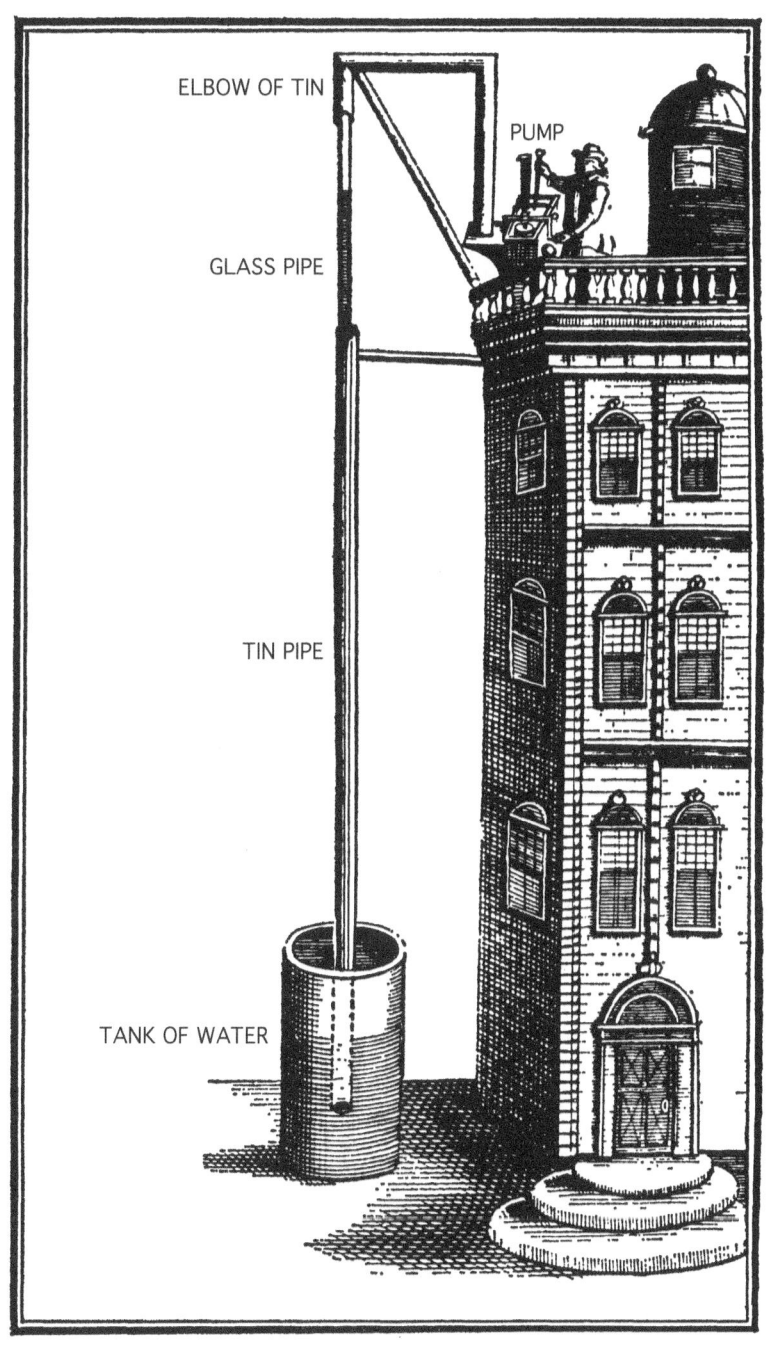

An out-of-doors experiment to find out how high Boyle's air pump could raise water. (From an old print.)

SEVEN

The Spring of the Air

THE FIRST published account of Robert Boyle's scientific work appeared in 1660, about six years after he had settled at Oxford. In it he described in detail the many experiments he had carried out with the aid of his air pump. The work bore the following lengthy title: *New Experiments Physico-mechanical, touching the Spring of the Air and its Effects. (Made for the most part, in a New Pneumatical Engine.)*

In this work Boyle gave a complete account of forty-three experiments made by him and his assistants. Some of these important experiments were discussed in the previous chapter; others will be explained in pages to follow. In the title of his work Boyle used the expression "spring of the air" because compressed air always tends to spring back and occupy a larger space when the pressure is decreased.

Anyone who has ever tried to force the piston of a bicycle pump down while a finger is held tightly against the outlet valve will understand what "spring of the air" means. Boyle himself noticed the "springiness" of the air in the barrel of his pump as the air was squeezed, or compressed. It had "bounce," yielded to pressure, and could be made to occupy a smaller volume. But the moment the pressure on it lessened, the air invariably bounced back. Later, this same observation of "the spring of the air" led Boyle to the discovery of his famous Boyle's Law.

With the publication of his first book, Robert Boyle became famous almost overnight. This work had a tremendous impact on educated people not only in England but also on the Continent and even among educated people in the American colonies. The book created a sensation because it revealed the ideas and methods of the New Science in a way which the general public could understand. Ideas were expressed in clear simple language by the author; the experiments themselves were what mattered, not the opinions of authorities or the complexities of logic. There was always a simple understandable cause for what happened in an experiment; and it was the business of a scientist to find this cause—perhaps by other experiments.

Boyle always wrote honestly of his difficulties and mistakes. There was no magic or mystery about his approach to science; he reported everything with what seemed the most extraordinary openness and sincerity. Above all Boyle had no use for the vague and wordy "philosophic" ideas which many scholars used to "explain" what they really did not understand.

The readers of Boyle's first scientific paper, or book, were people of education in all walks of life. They were impressed with Boyle's experimental approach and his search for simple explanations of how things in nature worked. Among Boyle's experiments that attracted a good deal of attention and interest were the transmission of sound in vacuums, the determination of the weight of air, and—of course—the barometer-in-vacuum demonstration which led to the discovery of Boyle's Law.

At the time of Boyle's work there was considerable controversy about how sound was transmitted. Was air necessary as a transmitter? If a sound is made in a vacuum, for example, would the vibrations be carried to a person listening outside the vacuum? Boyle arranged an experiment that he hoped would provide a definite answer to this question.

Boyle suspended a watch—in those days they were large and loud-ticking—in the middle of his receiver by means of a "pack-thread." In Boyle's own words, this pack-thread was "the unlikeliest thing to convey a sound to the top of the receiver." The receiver was then closed and sealed, after which it was observed that the sound of the ticking could be "plainly" heard by those "listening near the sides of it."

So far he had proved only that the sound of the watch got through to the outside when the receiver contained air. The next step was to start to pump the air out of the receiver. As the air was gradually exhausted, the sound of the ticking became fainter and fainter. Soon the experimenters were unable to hear any ticking at all, even when they put their ears to the sides of the glass receiver. They knew, however, that the watch was giving off sounds because the second hand could be seen moving as usual. Finally, "to satisfy themselves further," air was slowly let into the receiver. This caused the sound to increase until it was heard "at a two foot distance from the outside of the receiver."

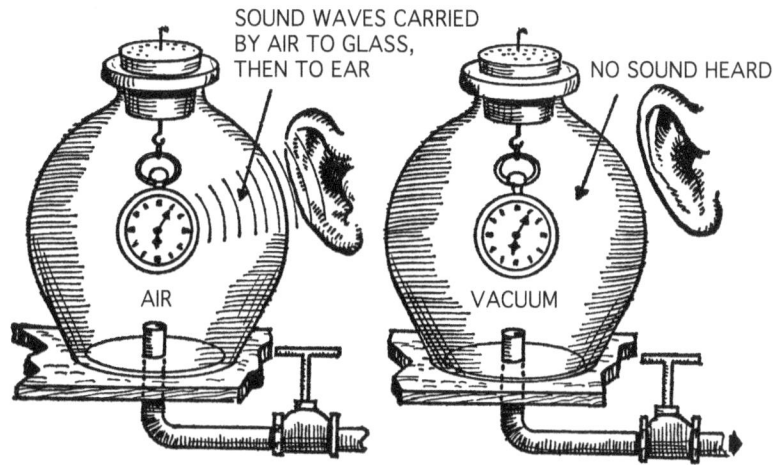

Left: Before exhausting air. Right: After exhausting most air.

Boyle showed typical caution in drawing his conclusions. The experiment seemed to prove "that whether or no the air be the only, it is at least the principal, medium of sounds." He tried similar experiments on sound transmission, using bells and ingeniously arranged clappers which could be operated from the outside; but his results were not as satisfactory as when he had used the watch. Evidently the larger contrivances managed to transmit the sound vibrations to the receiver and table despite the surrounding vacuum.

To prove that air has weight Boyle had to overcome many experimental problems. His contribution was a new way of demonstrating what had been known for some time; namely, that air, like any other substance, does have a definite weight. No one, however, had ever proved this directly by weighing a container of air in a space from which air had been exhausted. Since air is light, the upward push, or buoyancy, of the atmosphere interferes with accurate weighing. In other words, the air around the weighing pans pushes upward on those pans.

But now that Boyle had his air pump, he decided to prove directly that air has weight. He obtained a "glass bubble the size of an hen-egg," with a narrow stem extending from one end. The opening of this stem or tube was sealed so that the air in the bubble could not escape. Next came the job of balancing the "glass bubble" in one pan of a small scale against weights in the other pan. This, of course, meant that the scale or balance had to be taken out of the receiver every time weights had to be added or removed from the pan. After that, the scale was re-installed in the globe and the air pumped out once again.

Boyle now knew the approximate weight of his "glass bubble" of air in a surrounding vacuum. Then the "glass bubble" was removed from the receiver and a hole was made in the seal on its stem. After this, back into the receiver it went; again it was placed in the pan of the enclosed scale. Once more the receiver was sealed and the air was pumped out. Now Boyle was weighing a "glass bubble" with a vacuum in it in a receiver which also contained a vacuum. What did he discover? He found that the "glass bubble" weighed less the second time, that is, after its air had been removed. Here, of course, was direct proof that air has weight.

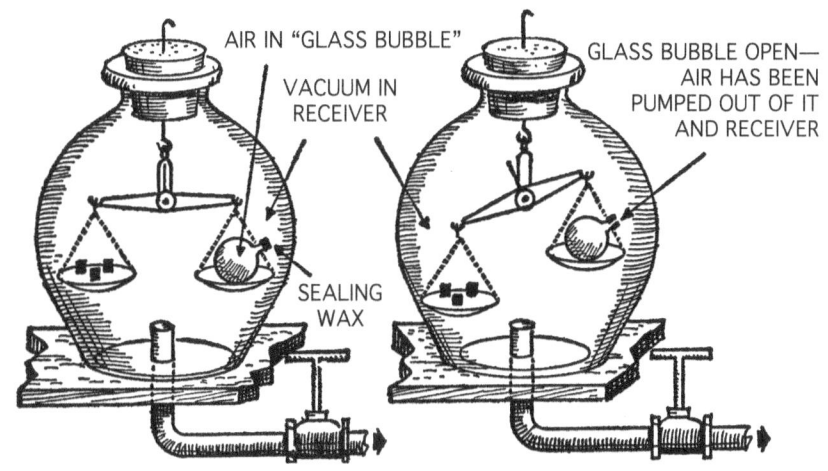

Proof that air has weight.
Left: Weighing air in an exhausted receiver. Right: Glass bubble has lost weight.

This experiment, however, did not give Boyle an *exact* figure for the weight of a known volume of air. In an effort to obtain more accurate results, Boyle now turned to another method.

He took a hollow copper globe with a nozzle attached to it. To remove most of the air from the copper globe, he heated it over hot coals for a few hours. The heat caused the air within the globe to expand and escape through the attached nozzle or tube. While the globe was still hot, Boyle closed the opening of the nozzle with a sealing compound; the airtight globe was then allowed to cool.

Boyle now had a copper globe from which most of the air had been driven out by heat. Then he weighed it; the cold copper globe, including the sealing material, weighed 6 ounces, 6 drams, 39 grains. Next he made a little hole in the seal, thus allowing air to rush into the globe. On weighing the globe again he found it to be close to 11 grains (about $\frac{1}{40}$ of an ounce) heavier than before.

Boyle wanted to find out how many times water is heavier than air. He already knew the weight of the air in his copper globe—about 11 grains. His next step was to determine how many grains of water the same globe would hold when filled. Now he had two figures—the weight of a particular volume or globeful of air, and the weight of the same volume of water. Thus he could compare the weight of water with the weight of air fairly accurately.

Boyle finally arrived at the ratio of 938 to 1. Galileo had tried a similar experiment and concluded that water is 400 times heavier than air. The accepted modern ratio is 773; a quart of water, for example, weighs 773 times more than a quart of air.

Robert Boyle's great book, *The Spring of the Air*, helped popularize the experimental approach to science. Here at last was a scientific work which everyone could understand. It revealed a new and exciting method of investigating nature. No longer did science have to be wrapped in mystery and long-winded discussions of causes. Boyle taught men to appreciate the experimental method.

Boyle's method of comparing the weight of air with that of water.

EIGHT

Boyle's Law

THE CIRCUMSTANCES surrounding the discovery of the famous Boyle's Law are interesting because they show how a scientist, every now and then, hits on something of great importance while engaged in an entirely different investigation.

Shortly after the publication of *The Spring of the Air* in 1660, a few criticisms of Boyle's work turned up amidst generous praise by scientists all over the world. One scholar in particular, Franciscus Linus, a Belgian physics professor at the University of Liege, offered an entirely different explanation of why the mercury stays up in a barometer tube. To Linus, Boyle's talk of the "springiness of air" was illogical and without experimental foundation. Incidentally, this was the same Linus who, twelve years later, also attacked Isaac Newton's treatise on the composition of white light.

This criticism did not disturb Robert Boyle, however, for he felt that the conclusions he had drawn from his experiments could not be disproved by mere words. It is true that Boyle liked to imagine air particles as a "heap of little bodies lying one upon the other, as may be resembled to a fleece of wool." These "little bodies" like tiny springs, "could be bent or compressed by the weight of the incumbent atmosphere." And when the pressure was removed or reduced, the particles of air would unbend and "stretch out themselves, thereby expanding the whole parcel of air." But it must be emphasized that Boyle himself did not regard the picture formed in his mind about air particles as of great importance. He could also think of the air in the manner of the French scientist, Descartes; namely, as whirling particles filling whatever space surrounds them. To Boyle a fact or an observation brought to light by an experiment was far more important than any theory attempting to account for that fact or observation.

At any rate, in due time, Boyle undertook to demolish his opponent's arguments. Linus had objected to the explanation of the barometer offered by Torricelli, Pascal, and Boyle—that the downward pressure of the atmosphere raised and held up the mercury in a barometer tube. To support his point of view Linus described this experiment: Take a long tube open at both ends, press the finger against the lower end, and fill the tube with mercury. Now place another finger on the upper end. Set the bottom part of the tube in a dish of mercury. Take only the lower finger away. Linus said that when he did this, there was a powerful pull or suction on the finger held tightly against the top of the tube.

Linus concluded that in the vacuum at the top of a barometer tube there existed an invisible cord, or *funiculus*. It was this cord, he said, that actually kept the mercury from falling out of the tube. In other words, the outside air pressure, in Linus' opinion, had nothing to do with the mercury barometer.

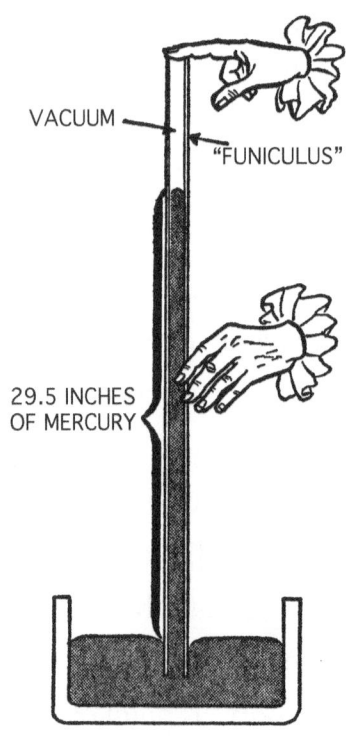

Linus claimed that a cord, or "funiculus," in a vacuum drew the mercury up and held it in place.

Boyle decided that the best way to answer Linus would be by an experiment rather than long letters in scientific journals. Therefore Boyle got busy and soon devised an experiment to prove the *funiculus* theory was contrary to observed facts. Specifically, he wanted to show that Linus' idea could not explain why liquids rose in tubes from which air had been pumped out; and furthermore, that Linus' *funiculus* could not explain what happened in the mercury barometer. As it turned out, Boyle discovered the relationship between the pressure and volume of gases—or Boyle's Law—while gathering experimental facts to answer Linus' criticism.

Here is what happened: Boyle took a long glass tube "crooked at the bottom so that the part turned up was almost parallel to the rest of the tube." In other words, he made use of what is now called a J tube, with the short leg sealed and the long leg open. He then poured a little mercury into the tube, enough to lock in the air in the short leg. By tilting the J tube he managed to get the same level of mercury in each leg.

This last condition was extremely important, for it meant that the mercury in each leg of the J tube was under the same

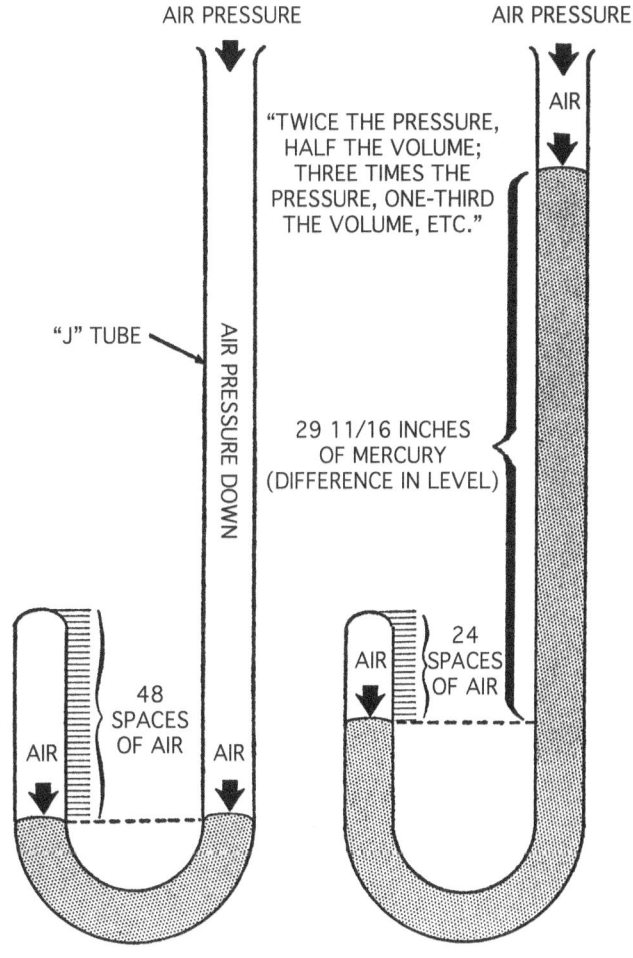

How Boyle discovered the law that bears his name. Doubling the pressure on a gas reduces its volume to one-half, provided the temperature remains the same.

atmospheric pressure. Thus if a tiny hole were made at the top of the short leg, nothing would happen—the mercury would not move and the enclosed air would remain where it was because the air pressure was the same in each leg of the J tube.

The mercury level of the laboratory barometer at the beginning of the experiment was $29\frac{1}{8}$ inches. Boyle then noted that the air in the short leg of the tube occupied 48 spaces of ruled paper. He then proceeded to pour mercury, a little at a time, into the long leg. The air in the short leg, compressed by the weight of the added mercury, bounced back slightly and then came to rest reduced in volume. Here was the "spring of air" which Linus claimed did not really exist!

As Boyle kept adding mercury to the longer side, he observed that the volume of air imprisoned in the short leg grew smaller and smaller. It was being compressed by the added mercury. He kept careful track of two measurements. The first was the difference in level between the mercury in the short leg and long leg, for this told him how much pressure was compressing the air in the short leg. The second measurement was the exact number of spaces, or volume, to which the enclosed air had been compressed. In short, every time Boyle added a few inches of mercury to the long leg, he stopped to take these two important readings.

He finally got the 48 original spaces in the short leg down to 24 spaces. When he measured the length of the mercury column, with "delight and satisfaction" he found it to be $29\frac{11}{16}$

inches above the mercury of the short leg. Now he could see it all clearly: this pressure added to the atmospheric pressure of $29\frac{1}{8}$ inches had succeeded in halving the volume of air in the short leg. In other words, the 48 spaces of air at a pressure of $29\frac{1}{8}$ inches of mercury had become 24 spaces of air at a pressure of $58\frac{13}{16}$ inches of mercury. Later, when Boyle studied the figures for the entire experiment he saw that a similar relationship between volume and pressure held for every pair of readings.

Boyle thus discovered one of the most important laws of gases. He observed that increasing the pressure on a gas reduces its volume. Doubling the pressure reduces the volume to one half; trebling the pressure reduces the volume to one third. However, Boyle was unaware that temperature, too, had to be considered. The modern form of Boyle's Law is this: The pressure which a given quantity of a gas at constant temperature exerts against the wall of the containing vessel is inversely proportional to the volume occupied.

Boyle had not forgotten, however, that Linus' arguments were still to be answered. This he did simply and thoroughly. Linus had claimed that the cord, or *funiculus*, was capable of holding up mercury in a tube to a *maximum* of 29 inches. Boyle merely put his mouth to the open end of the J tube and sucked some air out of it; a column of mercury about 50 inches long moved up the tube toward his mouth. The imprisoned air in the short leg helped by pushing outward when the pressure was reduced; and his lungs, acting like an air pump, did the rest.

That settled the debate. There was no mysterious *funiculus*, effective up to 29 inches. Air definitely had a "spring." It was the pressure of the atmosphere that held up the mercury in a barometer tube. Boyle, in a most gentlemanly, good-humored fashion, thus disposed of the arguments of his critic—and was quite satisfied.

Before concluding this series of experiments Boyle tried to find out if his law held true for reduced as well as increased pressure on gases. For example, would the volume of a gas double when the pressure on it was reduced by half? The ingenious Boyle soon got an answer to this question. He got a long tube, closed at the bottom, and filled it with mercury. In this tube he inserted a long "slender glass pipe the thickness of a Swan's quill." He sealed the top of the pipe while it was in mercury with a few inches exposed. By raising the sealed glass pipe while it was in the tube of mercury to higher and higher levels he discovered that the law held true. Reducing, or lessening, the pressure on confined air caused an increase in the volume of this air. In other words, halving the pressure doubled the volume of a gas.

The results of all this highly original work were published by Robert Boyle in 1662 as an appendix to the second edition of *The Spring of the Air*. He gave it this long title: *A Defense of Mr. Robert Boyle's Explications of His Physico-Mechanical Experiments, against Franciscus Linus.*

NINE

The Sceptical Chymist

IN THE SPRING of 1660, the year in which the first edition of *The Spring of the Air* appeared, Robert Boyle visited London to take part in the ceremonies welcoming King Charles II back to England. Oliver Cromwell had died two years before and his son, Richard, could not prevent the collapse of the Protectorate. The return of the King, so long exiled in France, marked the beginning of the period in English history known as the Restoration.

Robert Boyle was surprised to find that he had suddenly become famous. Not only were all the scientists in London talking about "vacuums" and the "spring of air," but the King himself asked for a private demonstration by Boyle. Boyle was offered a peerage but declined it; apparently he saw little value in having the title of duke or earl. He was also invited to enter into holy orders with the promise of a high position in the Church of England. Boyle refused this invitation politely, explaining that his only interest in religion was "to save his own soul." Evidently the Boyle family had managed to retain the esteem of Charles II, for titles of nobility were conferred upon two of Robert Boyle's brothers.

Boyle returned to Oxford in May of 1660, eager to resume his experiments, writing, and Biblical studies. He was upset, however, when he found the university in a state of excitement and disorganization, for the return of King Charles had

The King asked for a private demonstration of Boyle's experiment.

brought a change of policy and administration. Some of Boyle's close friends had been dismissed; others had decided to leave Oxford and settle in London.

It was obvious that there could no longer be any regular meetings of the "invisible college" in Oxford, since the members had scattered to different places. Boyle soon learned that meetings had been resumed at Gresham College, London, and that a plan for the establishment of a stronger and more formal society was being considered.

Boyle immediately threw himself into the task of creating a scientific society which would meet regularly to debate ideas, "promote the experimental philosophy," and in general further "the advancement of various parts of learning." A week after the plan was drawn up, Charles II agreed to become a *Founder* himself, thus signifying his wholehearted support of the new organization. A charter was granted in 1662 and the "Invisibles" adopted a new title—the Royal Society of London for Improving Natural Knowledge.

Though Boyle was tempted to move to London, he finally decided to stay in Oxford, which was close enough to the English capital for him to attend the meetings of the Royal Society. However, he soon lost his brilliant assistant, Robert Hooke, who in 1662 accepted the newly created position of curator of experiments to the Royal Society.

The year after his return to Oxford, Boyle published his most famous work, *The Sceptical Chymist*. A skeptic is one who is given to doubting; and Boyle, in this work, proceeded to challenge the basic ideas in chemistry of both philosophers and alchemists.

This important book became a milestone in the history of chemistry. In Boyle's time there was no science of chemistry as we know it today, but rather a craft called *alchemy* which was practiced for such useful purposes as extracting metals from crude ores, discovering drugs, making glass, distilling spirits, and preparing medicines. The men who studied these useful processes were called alchemists, probably from the Greek word *chémeia* (infusion) and the Arabic *al* (the).

The word "alchemist" today brings to mind a pseudoscientist who devoted his life to the hopeless search for a way of changing base metals like lead and copper into precious metals like gold or silver. While it is true that such a change, or "transmutation," was considered possible by alchemists, it is not true that these investigators accomplished nothing of scientific importance. From the tenth century right down to Boyle's time, alchemists added much to our knowledge of chemical processes. They performed experiments, gathered facts, learned valuable laboratory techniques, and discovered the properties of important metals and other substances. In addition, the alchemists found out how to prepare and use the three mineral acids—hydrochloric, sulphuric, and nitric.

Boyle was an alchemist and corresponded with the great physicist Isaac Newton, also an alchemist, about the possibility of changing mercury into gold. Such a possibility may sound strange to us, but for centuries men regarded transmutation as possible. Today, in our atomic reactors, transmutations of metals are indeed brought about when particles called protons are added to or subtracted from the nuclei of atoms.

Boyle's main purpose in *The Sceptical Chymist* was to transform chemistry into a science. He realized that the alchemy of his day was a mixture of vagueness and mystery, of fact and fancy, of truths and half-truths. It was based on ancient ideas, or hypotheses, inherited from the Greeks and medieval philosophers. The latter, despite the absence of experimental evidence, had accepted most of the theories of the ancient Greeks.

To change the craft or trade of alchemy into the science of chemistry therefore required destructive criticism. And Boyle, who had been drawn to the study of chemistry during his lonely years at Stalbridge, was well equipped to give it. After the weak supports of alchemy had been torn away, rebuilding with sounder materials could begin.

His first attack was on the secrecy and lack of clarity in the writings of the alchemists. He complained that the writers did not seem to care whether or not anyone understood them. Boyle objected to the common practice wherein highly regarded "physicians and philosophers" would "publish and build upon chymical experiments, which questionless they never tried."

Boyle also poked fun at the use of the vague expression "the chymists say, or the chymists affirm that," without bothering to supply information as to *who* said *what*, *when*, and *where*. In short,

Boyle wanted the chemists of his time to get rid of the mystery, loose thinking, and exaggerated respect for the ideas of the ancients. His plan was to draw "the chymists' doctrine out of their dark and smokie laboratories" so that they might be shown the "weakness of their proofs."

Boyle wrote *The Sceptical Chymist* in the form of a dialogue in which one speaker is a follower of Aristotle, another a spagyrist, or pupil of Paracelsus, a third expressed Boyle's own ideas, and a fourth served as a bystander or "guest." Boyle found this a convenient way of showing the superiority of the scientific method over both the mystical and purely intellectual approach to chemistry.

In this work the author proceeded to tear to shreds the ancient idea that had passed from the Greeks to the alchemists; namely, that the things or materials of the world were composed of earth, air, fire, and water. According to this theory, it was believed that one or more of these four *elements* were present in every substance. They also believed that the following was "proof" of its truth: When a piece of wood is burned, the four "elements" in it separate. The fire leaves the wood in the form of a flame; the smoke, a form of air, emerges from the burning wood and vanishes up the chimney; the water in the wood "boils and hisses" and in this way "betrays itself to more than one of our senses"; and the ashes which are left, "by their weight and fineness, and their dryness, put it past doubt that they belong to the element earth."

Boyle also stressed the fact that the followers of Aristotle's four-element theory never made clear what an "element" was. Fire, regarded as "a great opener of bodies," was supposed to break a substance down into simpler substances. Boyle then wrote of experiments he had performed where fire caused no changes at all in matter, as when gold or silver or a mixture of these metals was heated. He also noted that heating wood in a retort caused not simpler but more complex substances to be produced, such as "oil, spirit, sugar, water and charcoal."

Moreover, it was easy for Boyle to show that there was no general agreement among alchemists as to what was meant by each of the four "elements" of Aristotle. Fire was not the ordinary flame everyone was familiar with, but rather the "pure" element in the flame. Water was not mere water, but an ideal element responsible for the "liquidity" of substances. Air was not the air one breathed, but the mysterious substance capable of penetrating all matter. And earth was not simply earth, but the dry, weighty, unchanging part of every solid substance.

Boyle cited his own experiments to reveal the contradictions in the arguments of his opponents. He made fun of the reasoning of the "intellectual" chemists and pointed out the danger of building theories on ideas rather than on facts. All this, of course, was done in Boyle's characteristic style—with a gentle humor and light touch.

The scientist then turned his guns on the followers of Paracelsus, the famous sixteenth-century alchemist, whose teachings were highly regarded in Boyle's time. Paracelsus, born in Switzerland in 1493, had studied mining, medicine, and alchemy. He preached the value of experiment and observation, was critical of those who relied entirely on ancient books for their facts, and sought to apply his knowledge of chemistry to the treatment of disease.

Paracelsus began as a reformer with a strong faith in experiments as a source of knowledge. He believed in the four elements of the Greeks, but for practical reasons insisted that matter be regarded as consisting of *Three Principles:* salt, sulphur, and mercury. Here again, however, these principles were surrounded by magic and mystery. For example, the salt of the Three Principles was not ordinary salt, but the essence or "soul" of the salt. In the same way, sulphur and mercury were not the substances alchemists handled daily, but mysterious and all-powerful essences.

Paracelsus, who died in 1541, had urged alchemists not to devote their skills merely to the transmutation of base metals into gold, but to add to the knowledge of medical chemistry. Yet at the same time he himself believed in the "philosopher's stone" whose magic contact could quickly change metals into gold. He, too, kept seeking the "elixir of life," a miraculous medicine which would prolong life indefinitely. The teachings of Paracelsus, a fascinating and romantic character, continued to be revered by alchemists as late as the seventeenth century.

Boyle found it easy to poke holes in the arguments of the followers of Paracelsus—or spagyrists—as Boyle called them. He accused these alchemists of "playing with names at pleasure," of piling mystery on mystery. Boyle showed that many of the "experiments" made by prominent alchemists of his own period were not really experiments; rather, they served merely to bolster notions that were already believed in.

Concerning fire, the "great opener of things," Boyle pointed out that it sometimes caused substances to yield *less* than three principles and at other times *more* than three. He mentioned the fact that fire could not separate the gold and silver from a mixture of the two metals. On the other hand, the gold in the mixture could be extracted with *aqua regia*, which is a mixture of nitric and hydrochloric acids. How, then, could fire be used as a test for an element when it failed to distinguish between gold and a mixture of gold and silver?

What did Boyle hope to accomplish by this attack on the basic ideas of the alchemists? Simply this: He realized that there could be no true science of chemistry as long as no one understood what an element was. Chemistry needed a firm foundation of facts about the "multitude of bodies" in the world; the elements, he wrote, would be discovered only by constant seeking. In brief, Boyle was convinced that many elements—not just three or four—would be found among the innumerable mixtures and compounds of nature. Moreover, this knowledge could be gained only by using the experimental method. For this undertaking the opinions of scholars and philosophers were useless; experiments and only experiments would reveal the elements of the world.

And yet, if substances were not composed of *four elements* or *three principles*, then what *were* all "bodies" or things made of? This was a most difficult question to answer in the seventeenth century. Boyle first ventured to say what an element was *not:* "I...must not look upon any body as a true principle or element, but as yet compounded, which is not perfectly homogeneous, but it is further resoluble into any number of distinct substances, how small soever." In other words, it depended on the number of ingredients in a substance; if there were more than one, the substance must be a *compound*, or mixture, but definitely not an element.

What, then, *was* Boyle's definition of an element? It was this: "I mean by elements...certain primitive and simple, or unmingled bodies; which not being made of any other bodies, or of one another, are the ingredients of which all those called perfectly mingled bodies are immediately compounded and into which they are ultimately resolved."

Boyle, with typical honesty, admitted that he was not certain of how many elements there were in the world. He suspected that air was a mixture of various gases, or *effluviums*, as he called them. Gold and silver, he suggested, might well be elements, since countless experiments had failed to alter either of these metals in any way. He also offered the theory that the elements themselves, when discovered, would be found to consist of minute bodies or corpuscles whose grouping or arrangement served to make one element different from another.

What procedure, then, should chemists follow in order to find out experimentally whether or not a certain substance was an element? Unfortunately, this was something that Boyle could not tell them because he himself did not know how to identify an element. His advice to the seventeenth-century scientists was to analyze and keep analyzing until they were convinced that a substance could no longer be broken down. Not until a hundred years later did the French scientist Antoine Lavoisier develop the modern definition of an element as a substance which cannot be separated into simpler substances. By that time chemistry had advanced to a point where definite tests could be applied to a substance in order to determine whether it was an element or a compound.

Robert Boyle thus cut away a good deal of deadwood from alchemy so that modern chemistry could grow from its roots. His teachings had a profound influence on the chemistry of his century. He preached experimentation plus accurate observation. He warned against trying to build a structure of "reasonable" explanations without first laying a foundation of experimentally discovered facts.

Boyle further urged that chemistry be followed for its own sake rather than as an aid to medicine, mining, and the like. He warned against the tendency to oversimplify nature. Honest experimenting, honest thinking, honest writing—these were what he taught the chemists of the seventeenth century. For these invaluable contributions, Robert Boyle has gone down in the history of science as the founder of modern chemistry.

TEN

Flame and Air

EARLY in his career Robert Boyle developed an interest in the chemistry of burning. His absorption in this subject lasted practically all of his life. Again and again, he would return to the fascinating age-old questions: What is flame? What happens when a substance burns? What part does air play in combustion or burning?

Time after time the frail, tall investigator would try to forget his ailing body, weak eyes, and chronic tiredness by turning to the problem of combustion. We have already mentioned that he tried to burn a candle and a match in the receiver of his pump; in both cases the flames were quickly extinguished as soon as the air was exhausted. Apparently these "combustibles" needed air in order to keep burning, for he had observed that when air was allowed back into the receiver just before the candle flame died out, the flame would quickly revive.

Boyle soon decided that it would be better to start the burning not in the outside air but within the vacuum of the receiver. At first he attempted to set fire to the enclosed substance by means of a burning glass, which focused the sun's rays on whatever he wished to ignite inside the closed receiver. But this was not very successful because the thick glass wall of the receiver scattered the light rays, thus weakening their burning power.

Later, Boyle and his assistants hit on a better method. A red-hot plate was placed at the bottom of the receiver. Over the plate, dangling from a wire, was the substance to be burned. Working quickly, they pumped the air out of the receiver; then the wire was jiggled to make the combustible substance fall on the hot plate.

Using this method, they dropped sulphur wrapped in paper on the red-hot plate in the airless receiver. Boyle observed that the sulphur began to give off fumes, but did not catch fire as it did when heated in air. When the air was let in, however, "tiny flashes" were seen along with the usual bluish color of burning sulphur.

The behavior of gunpowder proved extremely puzzling to the experimenters. At first Boyle resorted to a burning glass to set off the gunpowder in a vacuum. It did not flash, but burned quietly only where the sun's rays were concentrated. Where the sun's rays did not strike it, the gunpowder did not catch fire at all. However, when air was let back into the receiver, the gunpowder went off with a flash.

Does gunpowder need air, as do other substances, in order to burn? Boyle was not certain. Then he got the idea of packing gunpowder into a goose quill. After setting fire to the end of this quill, he quickly plunged it into water. Boyle was amazed to find that the gunpowder in the quill kept burning even while it was

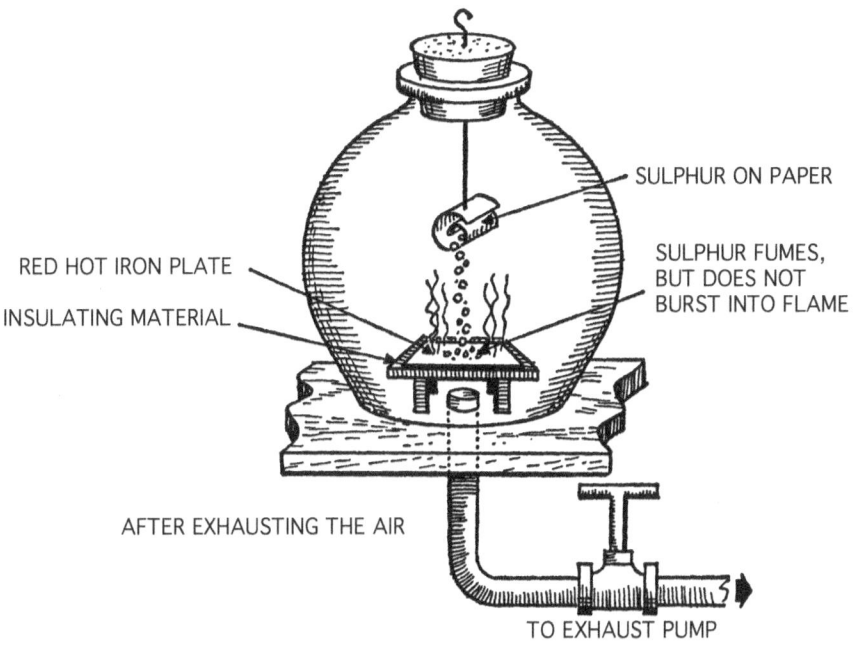

under water! Could it be that some air was mixed with the niter, or saltpeter—an ingredient of the gunpowder? Boyle went to the trouble of preparing crystals of niter in a vacuum, just to make sure that no air was mixed with this part of the gunpowder mixture. He repeated the experiment with the quill. Again he found that gunpowder burned under water!

What was the explanation? Boyle suspected that the niter gave off a "vapour" on being heated; and it was this "vapour" or "air," that made burning under water possible. Interestingly enough, this "air" or "gas" or "vapour" given off by heated niter was destined to provide chemists for the next hundred years with a clue to the nature of atmospheric air; the trail was followed by many investigators until Joseph Priestley and others finally discovered that saltpeter gives off oxygen when heated.

Boyle was not content with burning only solids in his vacuum. He tried the effect of a vacuum on burning gases—or "steams," as he called them. He poured "a saline and piercing liquor"—actually hydrochloric acid—on steel filings. The mixture became hot and gave off "steams" which he set afire with a candle flame. Boyle quickly lowered the vial with the burning "steams" into his receiver and proceeded to exhaust the air. At first the burning continued, but as the air in the receiver thinned out, the flame was extinguished.

Without realizing it, Boyle, like many other chemists of his period, had made hydrogen. It was not until 1766 that Henry Cavendish, another English scientist, investigated the properties of pure hydrogen. To Boyle, however, the important thing was that a peculiar kind of "air" or "steam," produced by pouring acid on steel filings, would not burn unless air was present.

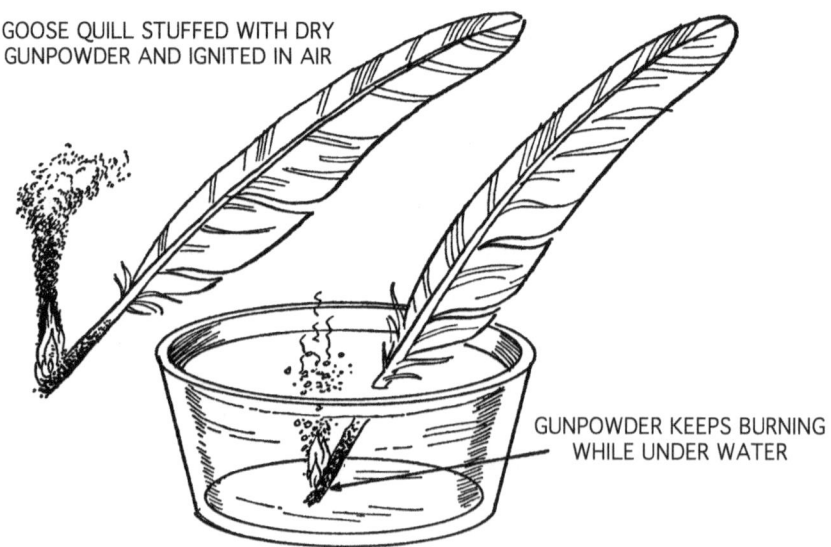

What exactly was there in air that was needed, and perhaps consumed, by burning substances? To this question Boyle returned again and again. Soon he began to think that atmospheric air "is not, as many imagine, a simple and elementary body, but a confused aggregate of effluviums"…and that "there is scarce a more heterogeneous body in the world." In short, the combustion experiments led him to believe that air was a mixture of many different ingredients rather than a single element.

In still another conclusion, Boyle came close to recognizing the role of the oxygen of the air in combustion—a discovery that was still about a century away. He noted that "the difficulty we find of keeping flame and fire alive, though but a little time, without air, makes me sometimes prone to suspect that there may be dispersed through the rest of the atmosphere some odd substance, either of a solar, or astral, or some other exotic nature, on whose account the air is so necessary to the subsistence of flame."

That combustion resembles respiration, or to put it another way, that the burning process is like the breathing process, was an idea which occurred repeatedly to Boyle during these experiments. He became more convinced of this resemblance as a result of his investigation of the behavior of a fly, a bee, a butterfly, a bird, and a mouse—each of which he placed in the vacuum of his receiver.

He observed, for example, how a fly in the receiver dropped from the side of that vessel "as if in a swoon" after a few strokes of the pump. The bumblebee was placed in the receiver along with a "bundle of flowers, which remained suspended by a string." The bee must have tried to hide in the corner of the receiver, for Boyle wrote that "we excited her to fly up and down the vessel till she lighted on a flower." The air was then slowly pumped out without, at first, any apparent effect on the bee. After more pumping, however, it fell to the bottom of the receiver, its wings motionless. The butterfly reacted in the same manner as the bee.

In the case of the bird, a lark, the experimenter noted that the creature was very lively at first, but as air was drawn from the receiver, it began to droop and look sick. Before long it went into convulsions and died. Boyle repeated the experiment with another bird, this time to find out how long it would remain alive in a sealed receiver. For about fifteen minutes the bird appeared to get along fairly well in the airtight container. After that the creature began to pant, keep its bill open, and show signs of distress. Boyle also observed the vapor on the inside wall of the receiver during this experiment; he suggested that these vapors, or "steams," made the enclosed air unfit for respiration.

The behavior of the confined mouse was similar to that of the lark. Very lively at first, it began to turn sick and acted giddy and weak as air was removed. In a short time the mouse, too, gave off visible "steams" and, like the bird, finally collapsed.

It occurred to Boyle, as he observed the reactions of the insects and birds and mice, that the extinction of life in animals was as certain and gradual as the dying out of a flame in a closed jar. Consequently, he began to consider the idea that the flame of life had something in common with the flame of a lamp. Both needed a constant flow of air in order to keep alive or burn brightly.

It must be remembered that Boyle lived at a time when nothing was known about the gases of the air, for these had yet to be separated and identified. Somehow, he suspected, "there is some use of the air which we do not yet so well understand, that makes it so continually needful to the life of animals." He assumed that the function of the air in breathing was to carry away the harmful or "recrementitious steams that are separated from the mass of blood in its passage through the lungs." This process, according to Boyle's view, could not take place in the rarefied air of a vacuum because there were not sufficient air particles present to carry the wastes away.

Like the other scientists of his century, he was unaware that the blood in passing through the lungs not only got rid of waste products but also acquired something from the air; namely, the gas we call oxygen. Boyle, however, came closer to understanding combustion than he did respiration. Also, his suspicion that the air "doeth something else in respiration" shows that he was not fully satisfied with his own explanation of the breathing process.

Boyle's investigation of flame and air inevitably led him to another problem whose solution had baffled philosophers and alchemists for centuries: What is the explanation of calcination? For nearly two thousand years it had been known that, with the exception of gold and silver, a powdery coating always forms on metals heated in an open bowl or crucible. If the heating is prolonged, many metals turn entirely to a powder which may be gray or white or brown or some other color, depending on the particular metal. This dross, or powder, was given the name *calx*, from the Latin word for lime; and the process by which it is formed was called *calcination*.

Now, according to the followers of Aristotle, burning implied that the element fire was leaving a substance. When paper or wood burned, for example, fire left these combustible materials; and what was left, the ash, obviously weighed less than the original paper or wood. The medieval alchemists "improved" on Aristotle by adding that "all that burns is sulphur"; in other words, the "soul" of sulphur escapes from every burning substance.

These explanations of burning were generally accepted until someone observed that in the case of most metals there is an *increase* in weight when they are burned or calcined. In other words, these metals *did not* become lighter. The alchemists now had a problem on their hands: Why should a metal like lead or tin become heavier when something *leaves* it? How could the departure of something from a burning metal cause an increase in the metal's weight?

One "explanation" was that the heating or calcination in open crucibles caused the "soul" of the metal to escape, thus making calx heavier. Another opinion was that the gain in weight resulted from the absorption of acids from the flame of the fuel. Finally, some believed that the fire itself, used to heat the metal, attached itself to the calx, or powdery material, during the heating process.

What was one to believe? Boyle attempted to find an answer. He heated and weighed quantities of various metals in open crucibles and, as expected, observed an increase in weight after calcination. Boyle even tried heating calcined metals and again discovered an increase in weight! His explanation—that the powders, or calxes, had been incompletely burned in the first place—seemed quite reasonable.

Soon he reached certain conclusions. Heating in an open crucible proved nothing because fumes from the fire could be absorbed by the hot metals. Why not calcine a known weight of metal in an airtight vessel or retort? In this way he could be certain that no external substance reached the hot metal. And if there should still be an increase in weight, then only one conclusion was possible: something had passed right through the glass of the retort and had been absorbed by the confined metal.

It must be kept in mind that even in Boyle's day, no one had any idea of the part played by air in combustion. Air was regarded as an elemental substance, and as such could not be broken down or separated into different parts. True, it had long been known that things would not burn unless air was present. But that, too, was explained by saying that air served to carry off the "sulphurous" vapors and heat from the burning substance. The discovery that air contained a gas called oxygen, which united with burning substances, was still many decades away.

At any rate, Boyle did as good a job as he was able, considering the state of chemical knowledge of his time. After experiencing difficulties caused by the bursting of glass vessels when heated, he got started on a crucial experiment. Boyle weighed out two ounces of tin, which he placed in a small retort "whose neck was afterwards drawn to a small apex." He then set the retort on hot coals so as to drive out as much air as possible through the small opening at the end of the long neck. After most of the air had been forced out of the retort, he sealed the opening by means of a flame.

Now Boyle was ready to calcine his tin. He set the sealed retort containing two ounces of tin on a bed of coals "far above two hours." At the end of this time he observed in the bottom of the retort "a gray calx and some very small globules which seemed to have been filings melted into that form."

Boyle removed the retort from the hot coals and let it cool a while. Then he cut off the long neck of the vessel and "heard the external air rush in, because, when the retort was sealed, the air within it was highly rarefied." (See diagram on facing page.)

He weighed the calx and debris formed from the tin on heating. It weighed 2 ounces and 12 grains. The results were definite: the tin *had gained* 12 grains, or about $1/36$ of an ounce, "by the operation of fire on metal." Boyle repeated the experiment, using other common metals. There was always a gain in weight when a metal was burned or calcined.

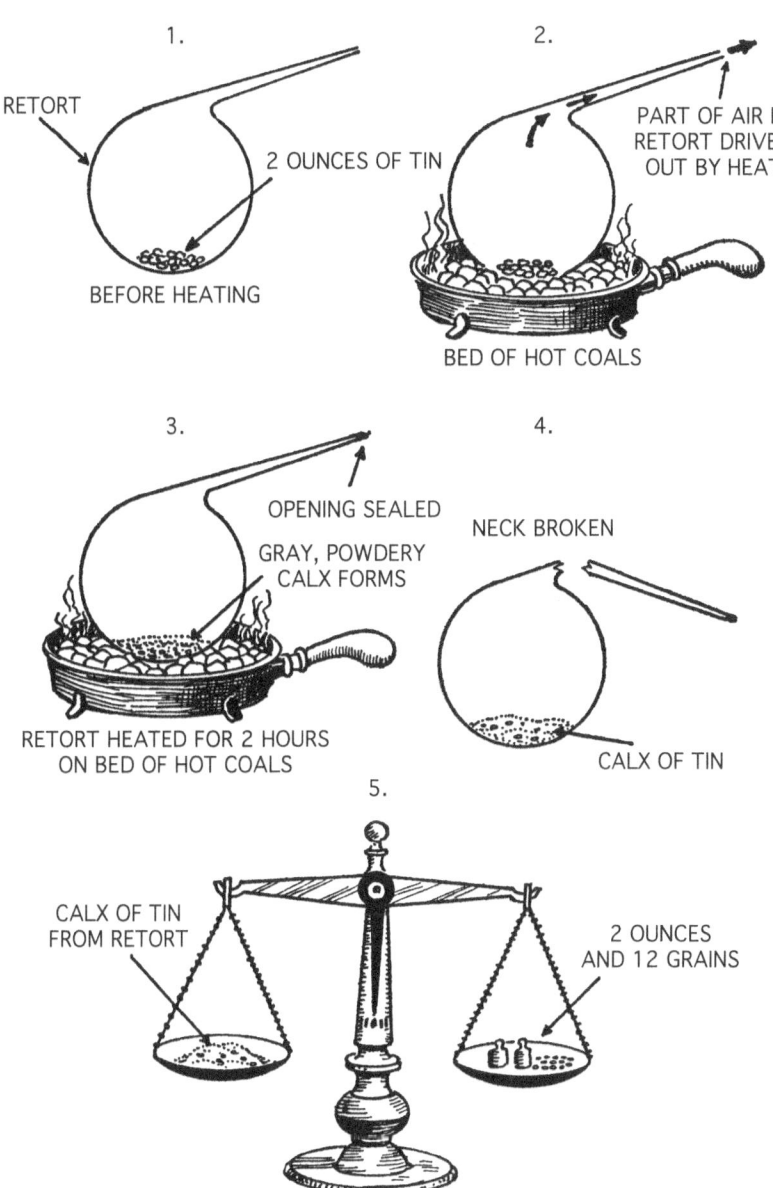

How Boyle heated tin in a closed retort.

What was his conclusion? Since there could not have been any absorption by the metal of fumes from the fire, Boyle reasoned, the fire material must have *passed through* the glass retort itself and been absorbed by the hot metal. And this proved that *fire had weight!* At the same time Boyle made the accurate observation that volume for volume, the calx weighed less than the metal; in other words, it had a lower density.

Boyle's incorrect conclusion that fire had weight was accepted by the chemists of his period; for a long time, it prevented the development of a better theory of combustion. That he had made a serious experimental error was soon pointed out to him by Chérubin, a French chemist. Boyle, however, was so certain that his experiment was foolproof that he paid no attention to his critics.

His mistake in the tin experiment was in not weighing the sealed retort *before* breaking the neck open at the end of the experiment. Because of this oversight, he never discovered that the retort and its contents weighed exactly the same after calcination as before. In brief, Boyle could have proved, as Lavoisier did about a hundred years later, that the gain in weight by the calcined tin was equal to the loss in weight by the enclosed air. The heated tin had merely united with the part of the enclosed air we now call oxygen.

ELEVEN

"The Christian Gentleman"

BECAUSE he was a truly religious man, Boyle began each day with morning devotions, after which he would spend long hours in the laboratory or library. There were always experiments to perform, books to complete, and reports to send off to the Royal Society. He would read by candlelight long into the night; and when his poor eyes became worse, an assistant was hired to read to him.

Every day presented the problem of pain, of overcoming the physical exhaustion which interfered with his work plans. Boyle always ate sparingly of the simplest food, consuming just enough to keep alive. He had long suffered from severe pains caused by stones in his kidney. Any illness which confined him to bed presented a fearful problem, for Boyle was convinced that lying down made his kidney pains much sharper. He always consulted a thermometer before going outdoors to help him decide what cloaks to wear; Boyle was convinced that a chill or cold or fever would bring on a host of other troubles.

Boyle's concern over his health was not unreasonable. He felt that there were definite causes for disease and that prevention was the wisest policy. He seemed, however, to have had no fear of death; like a true Christian, he felt that life in this world was of minor importance. But there existed in this world many things which fascinated the quick, creative mind of Boyle: experimental science, philosophy, religion, and literature. And if Boyle was determined to live as long as possible, it was largely because he wanted to accomplish as much as possible. Thus, the pale, drawn, scholarly Boyle took care of his weak body and made it last by sheer will power and endless attention to details of health.

Robert Boyle never married, despite efforts made by his sister and interested friends to arrange a suitable match for him. There were rumors, however, that he had once been interested in the beautiful daughter of the Earl of Monmouth and had written a romantic essay entitled *Seraphick Love* as a result of this attachment. This work, however, reveals a distrust of marriage, probably caused by an awareness of the unhappiness inflicted upon his brothers and sisters by his father's "practical" arrangements. Robert Boyle and his youngest sister, Margaret, were the only ones of the fifteen Boyle children who never married.

Throughout his life Boyle was as devoted to religion as to science. He arranged for eminent scholars to translate the New Testament into Turkish, Arabic, and even Malayan. As a director of the prosperous East India Company he managed to persuade his business associates to help spread Christianity in the Orient.

Boyle even had an Irish scholar translate the Bible into Gaelic in an effort to bring Protestantism to Ireland. But the Irish people had little interest in a Protestant Bible, whether in English or in

Gaelic. Quite understandably, they had as little use for the exported English religion as for the exported English army.

When Boyle unexpectedly received an additional grant of land in Ireland in 1662, he made up his mind to devote two thirds of the new income for the relief of the poor in Ireland as well as for the support of Protestantism. The remainder was to be used for spreading the Gospel in New England; that is, for missionary work among the American Indians.

Boyle, a lifelong student of the Scriptures, could see no basic conflict between science and religion. To him the scientific philosophy which made the universe out to be machine-like in nature and subject to the laws of mechanics was far from being Godless. Boyle insisted that even a mechanical universe needed the wise and ever-watchful care of God for its proper functioning.

Meanwhile, during his final years at Oxford, Robert Boyle had begun a series of experiments on heat, a subject about which very little was known at that time. His paper in this field, *New Experiments and Observations Touching Cold*, was published in 1665.

In order to investigate heat, Boyle needed an instrument with which to measure temperature accurately. The only such device available in England was Galileo's air thermometer, also called a "weather-glass" or "thermoscope." This device, which was invented by Galileo in 1592, consisted of a glass bulb with a long stem. After some of the air had been driven out of the bulb by heat, the end of the stem was placed in colored water. When the bulb cooled the air within it contracted, causing the colored water to rise part way up the long stem. A slight change in the temperature of the air surrounding the bulb would cause the liquid in the stem to rise or fall quickly. To take readings a strip of paper marked off into equal spaces or degrees was attached to the stem. These marks had no real meaning, however, because no one knew where to begin marking the degrees or how wide to make them.

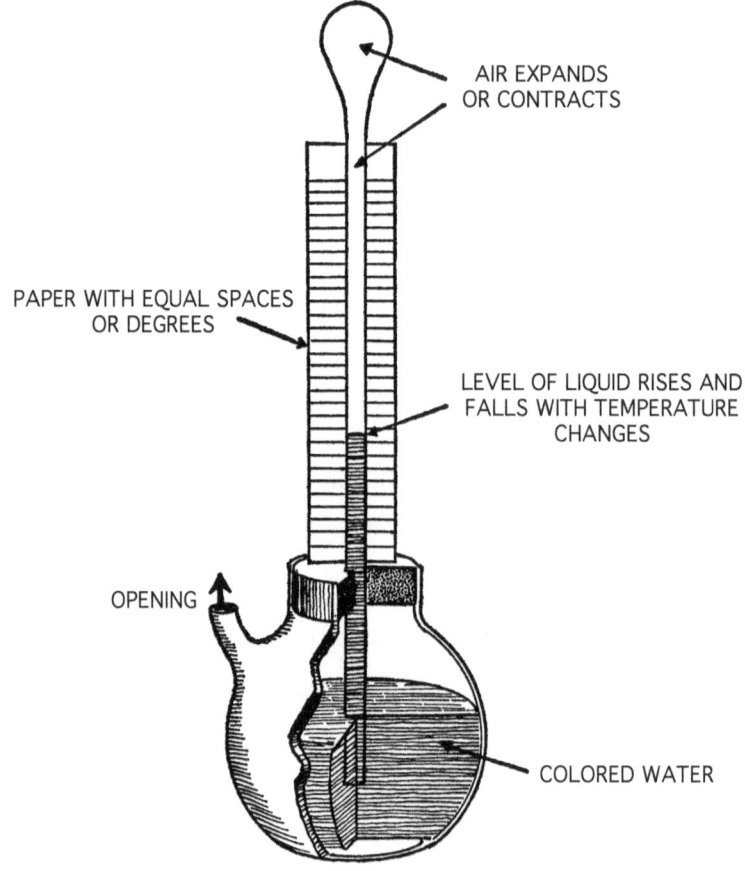

Galileo's thermoscope, or weather glass.

Before long, as a result of an improved knowledge of air pressure, it became clear that the weather-glass responded not only to temperature changes but also to variations in atmospheric pressure. In short, part of the rise or fall in the level of the liquid in Galileo's thermometer was due to temperature and part to air pressure.

Boyle tackled the problem of inventing a better weather-glass. He thought of making a "glass" consisting of bulb and stem only, partly filled with colored liquid and sealed. It would work, he felt certain, if there was a vacuum at the top of the stem; the confined liquid could then rise or fall without being held back by air in the stem. This sealed "thermoscope" could then be carried about without fear of spilling the liquid; it would also have the advantage of being free from errors caused by pressure changes.

As it happened, Boyle was shown a small thermoscope which a traveler had brought back from Florence, Italy. It proved to be exactly what Boyle had had in mind. The foreign thermoscope was small and used colored alcohol instead of water; the sealed stem was marked off into parts, or degrees, by means of small beads. The first of these sealed thermoscopes had been developed by Ferdinand II of Tuscany in 1641, but it took more than twenty years for the English to become aware of its existence. Using the Florentine model as a guide, Boyle set his glass blowers to work and soon sealed thermoscopes became common in England.

Now that he had a liquid in a bulb with a long narrow sealed stem, the next question was where to place the degree marks on his thermoscope. The liquid within responded to changes in temperature by contracting when cooled and expanding when warmed. Although each of these instruments worked, no two were alike because of differences in size, shape, and stem diameter. A mark of thirty degrees on one, for example, could not be regarded as the same temperature as the thirty-degree mark on another.

Boyle, along with Hooke and the Dutch scientist Huygens, soon came to the conclusion that a *fixed point* was necessary. By this they meant a starting mark which would be the same on every thermometer everywhere. Once they had determined the location of this mark, it would be possible to continue the markings up the stems by using the idea of each degree representing $1/1000$ of the volume of the liquid present at the time the first mark was made. To find this fixed point the thermoscope bulb would have to be placed in contact with a liquid or solid whose temperature was always the same.

Boyle wanted to use the *freezing temperature* of oil of aniseed for the fixed point, that is, the temperature of this oil at the moment it began to *congeal*, or *solidify*. Hooke preferred the freezing temperature of water as a fixed point. Huygens favored utilizing either the freezing or boiling temperature of water.

Although the method of marking off a thermometer on the basis of a single fixed point was an improvement, the results still left much to be desired. For example, the exact volume of a bulb was difficult to determine, and furthermore the degree numbers on one thermoscope could not be compared with the degree numbers on another. It wasn't until the end of the seventeenth century that Renaldini of Padua proved that *two* fixed points were preferable by far—one representing the freezing temperature of water and the other its boiling temperature. From then on, the problem became one of what numbers to assign the two fixed points so that the distance between them could be divided into a convenient number of parts or degrees.

Boyle now turned to experiments "with bodies capable of freezing others." He wanted to investigate the fact that "a mixture of snow and salt, tho' little used in England, is employed in Italy, and in other countries, to cool their liquors and fruits by immersing them therein."

He soon discovered that it was unnecessary to wait for cold winter days to freeze water. Glasses of water set in a mixture of snow and salt froze quickly. Boyle did not stop with salt and snow. He found that "several other things have the like virtue: alum, sal ammoniac, and even sugar may be substituted for common salt, tho' perhaps not to equal advantage." The modern explanation of freezing mixtures is that the freezing point of a solution is lower than the freezing point of pure water. In other words, the freezing point of water is lowered by dissolved substances.

Did water contract or expand when it turned to ice? In Boyle's day, there was much dispute over this question and it is easy to see why. If a bulb with a long stem, or "bolthead" as it was then called, was filled with water · and gradually cooled, the liquid in the stem kept shrinking or contracting. At that time no one had noticed the reversal or slight expansion of water that occurs near its freezing temperature. It was therefore assumed that the icy water kept contracting until it solidified. Cold, it was held, made all substances contract while heat caused them to expand.

Yet this was difficult to prove experimentally because the bulbs burst when the water within them turned to ice. The common explanation, or "vulgar doctrine" as Boyle put it, was that the sides of the bulb burst "to fill the space deserted by the shrinking fluid...for fear a vacuum should be left in the glass." Here again Boyle had to cope with the ancient "nature abhors a vacuum" idea.

Boyle was convinced that the bursting of glass vessels when surrounded by freezing mixtures was due to pressure from the ice that formed within. Moreover, he believed that the pressure of the air on the outside "trying to prevent a vacuum" had nothing to do with the bursting of the bulb. To prove this, Boyle very skillfully managed to freeze water in a glass vessel without breaking it. He got the idea from observing that water in ponds or lakes always freezes at the surface first.

Here is how Boyle accomplished this feat. He got a pail and packed its bottom with a mixture of salt and snow. After setting only the lower part of his bulb of water in this mixture, he filled the rest of the pail with unsalted snow. In this way he succeeded in freezing the water in the bulb from the bottom up. By allowing the liquid to solidify gradually, the upper part of the bulb's contents remained fluid long enough to be "capable of being impelled gradually upwards by the expansive force of the lower." Finally the contents of the bulb turned entirely to ice, rising "much higher in the stem than did the water before it froze." He had proved his point: water expands when it freezes. Vacuums had nothing to do with this phenomenon.

Once Boyle had succeeded in freezing water in a bulb, it was an easy matter to mark off the level of the ice in the stem; after that, the ice could be changed back to water by heating it. In one experiment he found that $91\frac{1}{8}$ parts of ice were formed from 82 parts of water. In other words, ice occupied about $\frac{1}{9}$ *more* volume than the water from which it formed. The modern figure for this increase in volume is approximately $\frac{1}{11}$; this is another way of saying that a cubic foot of water will yield 1.09 cubic feet of ice.

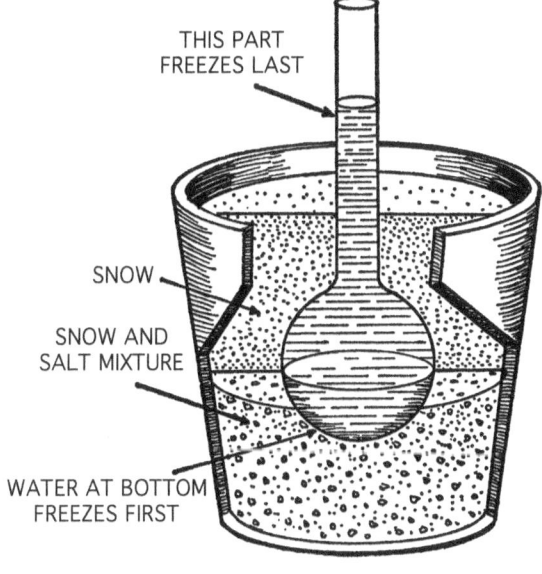

How Boyle showed that water expands when it freezes.

In another experiment Boyle tried to test the expansive force of ice when it forms from water. He prepared a hollow cylinder of thick brass, open at one end, "which was exactly fitted with a cover." His plan was to fill the brass cylinder with water, place the cover on carefully, set a hundred-weight on the cover, then leave it all outdoors on a frosty night.

The first and second attempts failed because the weather was not cold enough. Boyle decided not to depend on nature any longer: he applied a mixture of salt and snow to the outside of the brass cylinder. It worked! The patient experimenter got much satisfaction from observing that "one side swelled above the top of the cylinder, thereby raising up the cover, and threw down the weight."

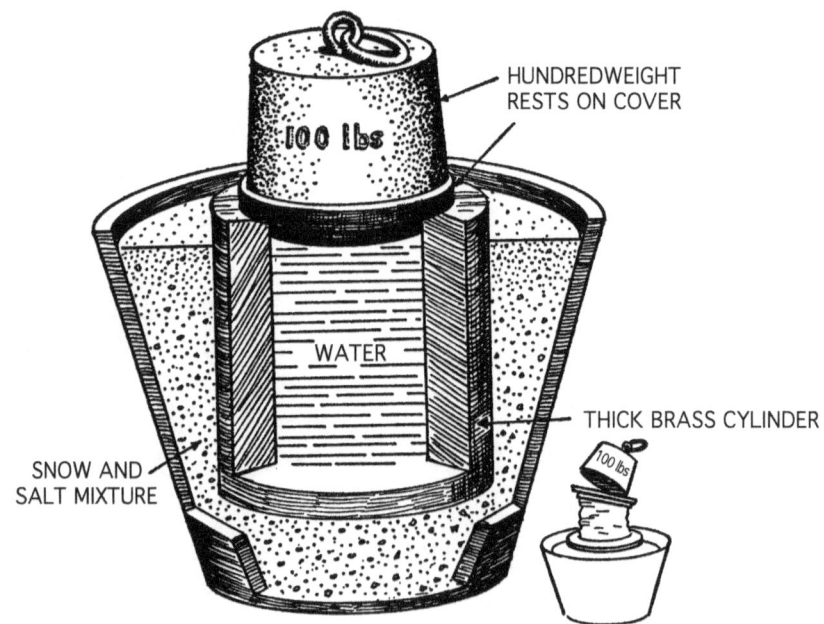

The expansive force of the freezing water raised the cover and "threw down the weight."

Not content with this, Boyle went on to perform a similar experiment with a gun barrel 14 inches long "whose bore was in diameter $3/8$ inch, and where least thick of metal $1/8$ inch, being filled with water, exactly closed at the breech and stopped with a screw at the mouth." On burying this gun barrel "in salt and snow for about two hours," he was delighted to see evidence of the enormous expansive force developed when water turns to ice. Boyle observed a crack six inches long "that ran obliquely from three inches above the breech and appeared widest at the middle."

In another interesting experiment, Boyle placed a small vessel containing lukewarm water in the receiver of his pump. After sealing the receiver, he proceeded to exhaust most of the air from it. Boyle was surprised to observe that the lukewarm water actually began to boil in the vacuum of the receiver. From this he learned that the boiling point of liquids was affected by the pressure of the atmosphere. In other words, reducing the pressure on the surface of a liquid enables it to boil at a lower temperature.

What actually *was* heat? This question in the 1670s was as difficult to answer as it had been at the time of the Greeks. Boyle believed, as had Francis Bacon before him, that heat was related to motion; that violent movement of tiny particles, of which all matter consisted, caused heat to appear; and that lessened movement of the same particles caused cold to appear. This view, of course, is close to the modern one, yet Boyle himself, as we have seen, had created confusion by insisting that heat had weight. Unfortunately, his faulty experiment in which tin gained weight on being heated had served to strengthen the ancient idea that heat was a material substance.

For a hundred years after Boyle this question—what is heat?—continued to plague chemists; it soon became a matter of vital concern in the development of chemistry. Even Joseph Black's experiments (conducted from 1759 to 1762), which finally succeeded in making a distinction between heat and temperature, did not establish the true nature of heat. It was then regarded as a material substance which penetrated the pores of bodies. When Count Rumford in 1799 proved conclusively that heat did not add weight to metals or other substances heated over a fire, the prevailing theory was altered to make heat into a weightless fluid. Even in 1789, when Antoine Lavoisier's famous *Traité de Chimie* was published, heat was listed in its pages as an "element" along with oxygen, nitrogen, silver, copper, and so on.

Gradually, this material theory of heat was discarded, thanks to the experiments of the Russian scientist Lomonossoff, the American Rumford, and the Englishman Davy. It was replaced by the modern conception of heat as a form of *energy*. That conception is often expressed as follows: Heat is the kinetic energy possessed by a body because its particles are in motion. Kinetic energy is energy of motion. It took a long time for this idea to become universally accepted, for even as late as 1837 books were being published by men who still regarded heat as a "weightless fluid."

TWELVE

Boyle Returns to London

AFTER eleven years at Oxford, Robert Boyle began to feel that he should change his residence to London. Not only had several of his friends moved to London but the metropolis had become the center of scientific activities. In addition, the Royal Society, of which Boyle was perhaps the most active and important member, occupied a good deal of his time. Since its meetings were held in London, Boyle had to make frequent trips there.

But, there was still the problem of where to live in London. How could he impose on his sister by moving into her house with his staff and laboratory? Also, the appearance of the "Black Plague" in London in 1665 caused Boyle to postpone his plans to move there. When it became evident that the Plague showed signs of spreading with frightening speed, the Court sought safety by moving to Oxford. The members of the Royal Society, too, scattered to escape the disease which was to take the lives of one fifth of the population of London.

With the Court temporarily established near him at Oxford, Boyle found his social obligations time-consuming and frustrating. The following year, when the Plague began to show

The Royal Society had become the center of English scientific activity.

signs of subsiding, he found a temporary residence in Newington, a suburb of London. Soon afterward, he changed to more permanent quarters in the city. The fact that few of his friends knew of his whereabouts indicates that Boyle wanted to be left alone to think and write.

About a year after the Plague, London experienced still another misfortune—the Great Fire in September of 1666. Boyle and his sister, both of whom were in the city at the time of this disaster, contributed their money and time to aid the many poor and homeless. During this period Boyle suffered frequent attacks of illness; this caused his worried sister to insist that he live in her house rather than by himself.

The strong-willed Lady Ranelagh had her way and did everything she could to make her Pall Mall house comfortable for her brother. This, of course, included arrangements for setting up his laboratory and housing his assistants. Boyle had many details to take care of before he could leave Oxford, where he had spent fourteen happy, productive years. Finally, in September of 1668, he moved into his sister's house in Pall Mall where he was to remain for the rest of his life.

Under Lady Ranelagh's patient care, Boyle, now a semi-invalid, continued to work in the laboratory in the back of the London house. He knew his body well and managed to keep up his strength and energy on a day-to-day basis. Boyle was always trying simple drugs, new and different ways of lessening his pains. Nor did he spare himself because of his many ailments;

each day was solidly packed with reading, writing, studying, and laboratory work. His mind remained eager and creative. He lived an exciting intellectual life, for to him ideas and knowledge and understanding were what made existence worthwhile.

His experiments on color while still at Oxford served to lead Boyle deeper and deeper into the science he liked best—chemistry. In London he began investigating the properties of acids and alkalis, as well as the fact that certain vegetable colors are changed by the action of each.

As a result of these studies, Boyle laid the foundation of what later became known as *qualitative analysis*—the branch of chemistry concerned with detecting, or finding out, what elements a given substance has in it. He observed, for example, that a strip of paper soaked in the syrup of violets turns red with acid and green with alkaline fluids. He pointed out that certain vegetable juices could be used as *indicators* to reveal the presence of acid, alkaline, or neutral substances.

Boyle also called attention to the fact that copper salts placed in a flame will cause the flame to take on a greenish color. In addition, the fact that a white cloud is produced when ammonia and hydrochloric acid fumes meet was known to Boyle. Further, he discovered how to test for a chloride by adding a solution of silver salts to bring about *precipitation*, or the formation of an insoluble white solid in the liquid if a chloride is present.

The story of how Boyle became interested in phosphorus is interesting because it shows how secretive alchemists could be.

Today it is difficult for us to understand how scientific knowledge could ever have been regarded as personal property. And it was precisely this centuries-old habit which Boyle tried so hard to reform.

It seemed that in the year 1669, a German alchemist named Brand discovered phosphorus while searching for the traditional philosopher's stone. News of the existence of a wonderful substance "that would shine in the dark" soon reached Johann Kunckel, a chemist in a neighboring town. Now Kunckel, eager to learn how to make phosphorus, went to Hamburg to ask Brand how he had accomplished it. The latter, to no one's surprise, refused to reveal his precious secret.

Kunckel then decided to try to discover the secret of making phosphorus himself in his own laboratory. Meanwhile, he had written to a friend, a Herr Krafft, telling of his difficulties with the stubborn Brand. Krafft himself then set out for Hamburg to try his luck with Brand, whom he hoped to persuade to part with the great secret.

Krafft reportedly paid Brand 200 thaler for the secret, with the understanding that Kunckel was to be told, if he inquired again, that the method of making phosphorus no longer worked. Here the matter rested until several years later when Kunckel published an account of some of the properties of phosphorus—without describing how he had prepared this element. The word phosphorus, incidentally, is derived from the Greek *phosphoros*, or "giving light."

The scene then shifted to England in the year 1680 when the same Herr Krafft visited the Court with samples of phosphorus to show King Charles II, an amateur chemist himself. In London Boyle was introduced to Krafft and in the course of a friendly conversation Boyle "imparted to him somewhat that I had discovered about uncommon mercuries." Apparently the German chemist was so touched by this confidence that "he confest to me at the parting," wrote Boyle, "that at least the principal matter of phosphorus was somewhat that belonged to the human body."

It seems that Boyle had heard of phosphorus and had either managed to prepare some of it with great difficulty or was still trying to do so. At any rate, Boyle considered the hint from Krafft very carefully and soon decided that the parts of the body most likely to yield phosphorus were the bones, urine, or hair.

Not long after Krafft left England, another German visitor mentioned to Boyle that "the degree of fire" was an important factor in the preparation of the long-sought-for element. Boyle wrote about this last remark that "when I reflected upon it, that was the only thing I wanted to succeed in my endeavors…"

Boyle set to work on the problem. He started with "a considerable quantity of human urine" to which, after evaporation, three times its weight of fine sand was added. The mixture was then "put into a strong retort" and heated for several hours, the fumes being allowed to condense in a vessel of water connected to the neck of the retort. At first the fumes bubbling through the water of his receiver simply disappeared. But soon the contents of the receiver began "to give a faint bluish light, almost like that of little burning matches dipped in sulphur." Eventually another substance "more ponder-ous than the former...fell through the water to the bottom of the receiver." In this manner, Boyle obtained the phosphorus he had been looking for.

Boyle, however, never regarded himself as the discoverer of phosphorus. In fact, in his writings, he states that there was some disagreement about who should be credited with "the first invention" of it. Some people, Boyle noted, believed that Krafft was the discoverer. Others favored Brand, "the ancient chymist dwelling at Hamburg"; while "by others again, the famous German chymist" Kunckel was thought to be the true inventor. Boyle himself had no desire to be involved in the dispute over priority, a matter, he observed, "I am neither qualified nor desirous to judge."

What interested Boyle most were the properties of phosphorus, which was sometimes called *noctiluca*, from the Latin meaning "shines by night." In his paper entitled *New Experiments and Observations Made Upon the Icy Noctiluca* (1681–82), Boyle brought many important facts about phosphorus to the attention of the scientific world. Air, he pointed out, had to be in contact with phosphorus in order for the latter to glow. He also noted the strong odor in the vicinity of phosphorus when it was exposed to air. Boyle discovered that this odor came from the air itself rather than from the fumes around the phosphorus. Today we know that phosphorus *oxidizes*—or unites with the oxygen of the air—to produce ozone, whose sharp odor is often confused with that of the phosphorus fumes.

Boyle also discovered that even a tiny quantity of phosphorus—one part in 500,000 parts of water—will produce a detectable glow. He tried dissolving phosphorus in various oils and found that the glow persisted in some and disappeared in others. White phosphorus, the kind isolated by Boyle, is of course dangerous to handle, for it is not only extremely poisonous but also catches fire spontaneously when exposed to air. For this reason, white phosphorus is always stored under water.

For Robert Boyle, the great obstacle to the growth of the science of chemistry was the secrecy of the alchemists—of which the phosphorus story is but one example. He disliked this foolish or childish attitude and fought it all his life.

Indeed, Robert Boyle became the outstanding preacher of the New Learning. This meant that he advocated the sharing of ideas and information, open discussion of conflicting views, and the use of clear and simple language by scientists. Boyle realized that scientific progress did not depend merely on the application of the experimental method. It was also necessary for scientists to inform the world of their discoveries. In this way, man could build on the work of others.

Robert Boyle practised what he preached. Whatever he discovered himself was immediately published by the Royal

Society for all to read. Nor did Boyle hesitate to investigate sciences other than chemistry in order to contribute new knowledge.

In Boyle's time, most of the separate sciences were all part of what was termed natural philosophy. Thus it was possible for a man like Boyle to know all there was to know about several sciences. Although Boyle's most important contributions were in the fields of chemistry and physics, he was also deeply interested in electricity and physiology. Two minor experiments of Boyle, one in each of these sciences, show that he was indeed a well-rounded "natural philosopher" of the seventeenth century.

In one of them, Boyle described the electrification of hair by friction. He noted that locks of false hair from wigs, when dry, "will be attracted by the flesh of some persons, as I have proof in two beautiful ladies who wore them." He observed, also, that these ladies "could not keep their hair from flying to their cheeks, and from striking there..."

Ever curious about such mysteries of nature, Boyle immediately resorted to an experiment. At his request, one of the ladies removed a false lock, which was then suspended in air. Boyle then asked the gracious but lock-less lady "to hold her warm hand at a convenient distance...as soon as she did this, the lower end of the lock, which was free, applied itself presently to her hand."

It must be remembered that although William Gilbert's great work on magnets had been published in 1600, very little was known about frictional electricity. Scientists believed that some substances, like amber, glass, sulphur, and sealing wax, could be electrified by friction; other materials, like ebony, flint, pearl, and the metals, could not be given an electric charge by rubbing. It was not until the next century that Gilbert's classification of substances, as either electrics or nonelectrics was shown to be incorrect; even metals, for example, could be electrified by rubbing—provided they were well insulated.

The physiological investigation carried out by Boyle was on the function of membranes in the human body. He became interested in this subject when an opportunity presented itself in the form of the semi-exposed heart of a distant relative. This gentleman had an open thorax as the result of a wound suffered during his youth. Through this opening, or "window" Boyle could see the pulsating heart, over which the owner would every now and then cheerfully squirt "some warm medicated" liquid. Fortunately, the hardy relative had adjusted to moving about with an open thorax, and not only lived for a long time but even served his king as commander of an army.

These last two interests of Boyle serve to call attention to one of his most appealing characteristics—the bright, almost boyish curiosity that he retained all of his life. He was fascinated by everything in what he called the "book of Nature"; the physical world was forever exciting to him because it was full of questions, problems, puzzles. To the end of his days, Boyle remained certain that there was a grand pattern in nature, and that science could discover this pattern by applying the experimental method.

THIRTEEN

Courageous Invalid

In 1670, two years after he had moved to his sister's house in Pall Mall, Boyle suffered his first paralytic stroke. For eleven months the stricken scientist was unable to move from his bed. At the end of this time, he succeeded by sheer will power in forcing his muscles to serve him once more.

An eagerness to try new things as well as a natural optimism must have been responsible for Boyle's partial recovery. He was a man who refused to give up. He massaged his own feet and legs with various preparations and ointments; he used new and unusual medicines that he prepared himself. To get as much fresh air as possible, he had himself carried to his coach daily for a drive. In addition, he invented exercises to strengthen the muscles of his arms and hands and legs.

Nor did Boyle neglect his mind during this painful period, for he had his assistants read to him daily. In addition, they would take down the ideas that he dictated—including directions for experiments. Boyle, as it turned out, was far from through with life; he still had much to think about and to do. In the years following his first stroke, many important books and papers came from his pen.

After his almost miraculous recovery, Boyle very sensibly began to restrict his activities. For example, he became less active in the affairs of the Royal Society, the East India Company, and the Society for the Propagation of the Gospel. At this time, the stream of visitors from all over the world who came to visit him in London began to be a burden. They came because Boyle had achieved an international reputation as a scientist and scholar. After his illness, in the hope of preserving his precious time and energy, he let it be known that he would receive visitors only on certain days of the week.

Much of Boyle's writing during the latter part of his life was devoted to combating the idea that the New Science was atheistic, or that it encouraged people to doubt the existence of a Divine Creator. Time and time again, the invalid would dictate arguments which he hoped would convince suspicious clergymen that one could be a scientist and true Christian at the same time.

To Boyle, the marvelous arrangements and adjustments found in the simplest plants and animals were evidence of the existence of God. He, like the great Isaac Newton, was not at all fearful that science would someday replace God with a mechanical world; both men believed that God had created the entire system of the world from the very beginning. Moreover, Boyle had a deep-rooted feeling that beyond the facts and ideas gathered by scientists are matters the human mind simply cannot grasp; that where reason is useless, faith in God is necessary.

Robert Boyle's gentleness, honesty, and unselfishness impressed all who knew him. Even in arguments over matters which meant a good deal to him, Boyle never insulted, abused, or ridiculed his opponents. He never cared for fame or high office. All in all, Robert Boyle was an unusually reasonable man, perhaps because his clear, peaceful mind was seldom troubled by vanity, envy, or anger.

Indeed, all of his life Boyle remained certain that the church he had been born into—the Church of England—was superior to all others. Because he felt so sure of this, Boyle during most of his lifetime displayed a missionary enthusiasm in his efforts to "bring light" to heathens, atheists, Jews, Protestant dissenters, and Roman Catholics. Yet even here the disagreement on religious matters was intellectual in nature and based on a desire to help people "see" what he regarded as the truth. Truly a man of peace and good will, Boyle was always an open foe of religious intolerance.

Gradually Robert Boyle's occasional communications to the Royal Society ceased because of his failing health. Boyle, offered the presidency of the Society in 1680, had refused this honor because it involved taking an oath of office, which was against his religious principles.

In 1691, both Boyle and his sister became seriously ill. Realizing that the end was not far away, he arranged his affairs and drew up a will, one of whose provisions established the famous Boyle Lectures. This provision set aside an income of fifty pounds a year to pay the salary of some outstanding minister who was to preach eight sermons annually "for proving the Christian religion against unbelievers."

Lady Ranelagh died on December 23, 1691. The loss of his beloved older sister, whose devotion and companionship had brought him so many years of happiness, was a great shock to Robert Boyle. The blow apparently broke the delicate thread that had for so many years attached him to life. He was tired of fighting pain and weakness. Boyle himself passed away a week after his sister's death. Brother and sister were both buried in the chancel of St. Martin's-in-the-Fields, which faces what is today Trafalgar Square in London.

Thus ended the remarkably useful life of one of the great teachers of the seventeenth century, the "saint and scientist," the preacher of experimental philosophy, and the founder of modern chemistry.

Beloved and respected by all men, Robert Boyle helped to set science on the productive course it was to follow during the next three centuries. In the Preliminary Discourse of his *Philosophical Works*, Boyle described his own contributions to science in these simple and humble words:

I COULD BE CONTENT THE WORLD SHOULD THINK I HAD SCARCE LOOKED UPON ANY OTHER BOOK THAN THAT OF NATURE. I ALWAYS ESTEEM HIM THE MOST PROFITABLE AUTHOR, WHO DOES NOT ENDEAVOUR TO SHOW HIS OWN LEARNING BUT TO INCREASE THE KNOWLEDGE OF HIS READER.

www.ingramcontent.com/pod-product-compliance
Lightning Source LLC
LaVergne TN
LVHW041854070526
838199LV00045BB/1592